C
IVF and Us

RACHAEL MOODY

AMBASSADOR INTERNATIONAL
GREENVILLE, SOUTH CAROLINA & BELFAST, NORTHERN IRELAND

www.ambassador-international.com

God, IVF and Us

Paperback: ISBN: 978-1-64960-194-0

Cover Image by Sarah Cameron
Printed in UK

Ambassador International
Emerald House
411 University Ridge, Suite B14
Greenville, SC 29601
www.ambassador-international.com

Ambassador Books and Media
The Mount
2 Woodstock Link
Belfast, BT6 8DD, Northern Ireland, UK
www.ambassadormedia.co.uk

Contents

1
Waiting

Isaiah 40:31

"But they who wait for the Lord shall renew their strength; they shall mount up with wings like eagles; they shall run and not be weary; they shall walk and not faint."

I've heard it said that if God takes you on a journey or gives you a story, then you should share it. This is my amateur attempt at doing so. Our story is no spectacular, or no worse or better than anyone else's but hopefully someone going through a similar rollercoaster will be encouraged and take comfort. Or maybe this will be useful to anyone who wants a glimpse into the journey or to find out more about fertility struggles. Our story is just one story of IVF and everyone has different experiences but even putting disjointed thoughts on paper may help me process the past few years.

Waiting.... Hard to do and frustrating to endure, especially for someone as impatient as me. I have always known I would love to have my own children, however I never really believed that I would get married. I guess I had low self esteem that I never thought that anyone would ever choose me to spend their life with. But, along came Mr Moody and that was the beginning of a bright new chapter of fun and adventure when we married in February 2015. I have always had a strong desire to foster or adopt children as well as have my own and very much saw and still see this in my future. Of course Phil and I talked lots before we got married about the important topics to ensure we were on the same page. We both were keen for children as soon as possible as we wanted to have 3 or 4 but for some reason I was always realistic and upfront about the prospect and kept saying "if we can", "we can't take it for granted", even though in my mind I was praying there would be no issue and we could have the family our hearts desired.

We were also keen for twins (I'm sure the reality would be far different from the dream) and I was hopeful as they run in Phil's family! I also shared my desire to help kids who had no homes. I strongly felt why would we not open the home that we had been blessed with in this regard. Phil agreed he was open to the prospect in the future but wanted to try for our own biological children first. I had to respect that and I was just glad that it wasn't a 'never' from him as it was such a strong desire for me it would have been a potential deal breaker. Children in our lives in the future was a natural desire for us but we trusted that *"Children are a gift from the Lord; they are a reward from him"* Psalm 127:3. We would have to just surrender our desires to Him. It was not a certainty as God's ways are higher than ours.

I had bridesmaid duties in the first few months of getting married and we talked about starting our family soon after that. Time passed and we tried not to get anxious about it but deep down I was thinking what if there is an issue as the waiting lists and referrals can take so long and I was now in my 30s. This didn't quite fit with my timeline of events but we had to surrender it to God. His ways are perfect. We continued to pray and fill our lives with busyness. Spending time with family and friends, following our different interests in hockey, gardening, crafting, house decorating, taking weekends away, beach walks and holidays with friends and family, trying to enjoy this child free time. Looking back, we became and still are, very busy people, blessed with many opportunities to meet up with people and fill our time with distractions. Phil always remained upbeat but I was always thinking we need to move forward if something is not working out and get a plan together. I can cope better if there is a plan in place ahead but if it's all too unknown then anxiety can be overwhelming. I would be content as long as I was on some kind of journey involving having children in our home, rather than none, whatever the road looked like.

In December 2016 I asked for a referral to the Regional Fertility Clinic, a regional clinic in Belfast covering all of NI for initial fertility issues, linked to the Royal Victoria Hospital. During this time we spent a small fortune on pregnancy tests, ovulation sticks and waited patiently and expectantly. Every month more and more boxes of tissues were used as emotions became stronger but still a sense of peace remained that God was in the waiting. After all, He understands waiting. Jesus waited. Waited 33 years to die so we could have life. Despite His wait, He lived life fully in the midst of it.

2

Plan B

Psalm 46 v 10

"Be still, and know that I am God; I will be exalted among the nations, I will be exalted in the earth."

We soon learnt that marriage isn't a fairytale or a Disney movie. The rollercoaster of emotions can be intense and none more so than when faced with a trial of any kind. Plan A was not working for us so Plan B it was then. We had 2 initial appointments at this regional clinic in March 2017 where we both had to attend. The worst case scenario we thought before we went in was that

(1) - we would be told we could never have children or weirdly enough

(2) - that we would be told there was nothing wrong.

In my mind if we were told that there was no issue then we would not get any help, there would not be a plan and this waiting and stress would just continue. We sat there in mutual silence watching other couples barely conversing or making eye contact in the waiting room. Everyone knew why we were all there yet there is a silent embarrassment about the whole situation. We were all naive, completely clueless as to what was going to happen when we went through the security coded doors and about to start this new chapter. I decided that day that I would try and document this journey wherever it was going to take us with some photographs. Although, all I could manage that day was a photo of our feet in the waiting room, an attempt to be arty and emotive but it failed.

The consultant was nice enough but very matter of fact (you could tell he had done this a thousand times) and empathy was not overly strong but we appreciated the honesty. He told us that the test results showed that there was an issue with one of us in particular that we would not have ever been aware of, if it wasn't for these specific tests. Science blew my mind and this was only the start of it all. The loss of dignity began for both of us with these assessments as well as the relentless efforts at drawing blood. To be told the news in black and white that day was both relief but also gutting. It was the realisation of what we both knew buried deep down that if we wanted a family, then we would need some help. It wasn't impossible on our own but there was a low chance of success. Although we won't forget that day when our fear became realised, we knew God was able and nothing is impossible. Although it was not our chosen path, God had us here on a detour for His reasons. He has got the whole world in His hands, including us and even the little tiny baby so why wouldn't His plan be for good. We were sent away with a booklet on something called ICSI, a counselling leaflet and a new appointment for a few weeks later and told to do some research and decide if we wanted to formally go on the waiting list, weighing everything up. In Northern Ireland there is only one free chance at IVF on the NHS compared to some areas of Scotland and England where couples may receive up to 3 rounds. It remains a postcode lottery. Although with Stormont up and running again, the need for more free opportunities remains on the future agenda. The alternative was to pay privately and be seen quicker but we thought we needed to save for this (around £6000 at the time) and we would see what this free round would bring. If extra eggs were gained, they could be frozen with the NHS round and used in the future so we were hopeful for this also.

So began a whole new world of internet searching, full of acronyms, stressed out women and language I did not understand with everyone sending 'positive vibes' and wishing for 'baby dust'. It was a world we didn't want to be in but here we were. We had officially joined the 1 in 8 club who had fertility difficulties. We were thankful that God was bigger than this and had it all under control and we could rely on Him rather than comments on forums and wishful thinking. Plenty of forums and internet pages both educated and scared me. ICSI is a form of IVF that we required, a more detailed version. Intracytoplasmic sperm injection (ICSI) is an in vitro fertilization (IVF) procedure in which a single sperm cell is injected directly into the cytoplasm of an egg. The who into the what now? Complete gobbledegook but we trusted the professionals and more importantly God. The IVF/ICSI procedure and various research is outlined factually on websites such as nhs.uk and hfea.gov.uk (Human Fertilisation & Embryology Authority). They outline the 6 main stages of the IVF process as being...

1. Suppressing menstrual cycle with medication
2. Stimulating egg supplies
3. Progress monitoring and egg maturity
4. Egg retrieval
5. Egg fertilisation
6. Egg transfer

Statistics are difficult to interpret as there can be many factors and variables but the NHS gives general statistics (live births as a result of IVF treatments between 2014 and 2016) was found to be:

29% for women under 35

23% for women aged 35 to 37

15% for women aged 38 to 39

9% for women aged 40 to 42

3% for women aged 43 to 44

2% for women aged over 44

It was important to also consider the risk factors that may raise their head during the process such as uncomfortable side effects from medications, dangerous multiple births, ectopic pregnancies and early miscarriage, and an illness called Ovarian Hyperstimulation Syndrome (OHSS).

Despite the medication, injections, procedures, side effects and emotional and mental toll ahead, we signed up for the waiting list 2 weeks after the initial appointment. At that stage we were told the wait would be 9 months but we secretly hoped this was an overestimate! During this time, there was a scare amongst the infertility community when there was a media awareness campaign that they might put on hold all fertility treatment in Northern Ireland due to the collapse of Stormont. We were so close to being top of the list yet this could all derail everything. This was a tense time as we waited to hear the outcome. Things still proceeded in the end but the whole process of waiting was extended to 11 months. In Feb 2018 we finally got the "top of the list" letter to go for our initial consultation at the Hospital this time. Back to another waiting room of counselling help-line leaflets, nurses looking at you with pity and more waiting for your name to be called to receive further medical jargon and sympathy. This was a quick blood appointment so nothing too taxing. Two weeks later again we met the nurse to talk through the protocol and explain all the medication in the 2 hour appointment. She was very direct , like matron old school direct but we came away with a blue hospital bag of medications unsure of what to do and feeling slightly guilty after a telling off for not taking enough folic acid. "He knows better than I, He knows the way, I've let go the need to know why but He knows better than I" - this lyric from the Joseph movie soundtrack kept floating around my head. We waited for our specific day to begin the medication, typically the first day fell when we were away for our anniversary, 3 years after the happiest day of our lives, we were excited to start another chapter.

3
Conflicted

Philippians 4 v 6

"Do not be anxious about anything, but in every situation, by prayer and petition, with thanksgiving, present your requests to God."

Despite our decision to proceed with the IVF style treatment, there were still conflicts felt (some still remain) in relation to was this Gods desire for us and how would we know? What was the view of Christianity and assisted reproduction? Did God put the desire in my heart for fostering and adoption because we would never have children? How many times should we try IVF before letting it go? Was it even Biblical to go down this route? I knew no one who was going through fertility treatment that had said. Most of my close friends had children and I especially had never heard of IVF discussed in Christian circles so I was confused. I felt that some parts such as egg donation, surrogacy and genetic selection were not for us at this time but we were at peace about receiving medical help for our situation which we saw it as.

Some people feel that IVF would not be for them and if they were in the situation then they would adopt or be content if this was God's desire for them not to have children. We prayed if God did not want to take us any further on this journey then the door would be clearly closed at any stage and obviously so. We still pray that prayer though it is difficult to listen for the answer especially if it is one that you don't want to hear. We felt that our fertility struggles were medical, there was a clear reason for it so in our perspective, we were seeking treatment for this.

We had to be careful as we had much paperwork to sign and were encouraged to donate eggs if we could to help other women but we felt that this was not a route we were at peace with at this time but everyone is different. Very little is said about IVF and Christianity that is clear. We have learnt that it comes down to a personal faith but opinion that can be conflicting and divide Christians on the controversial matter. Obviously some religions see assisted reproduction as sinful but we felt that God had given us an overall peace about this journey we were on despite natural conflicts in our human thoughts. The journey became as much a spiritual one as it was physical, mental and emotional. Where did IVF sit on the moral compass for us?

The major moral conflict that unsettled us was the outcome for the embryos that are not used and at what stage does life begin? I don't have all these answers but we decided that we would try and freeze as many embryos as we could allow for to be used by us ethically in the future and God would take care of the rest if we surrendered it fully into His hands. We can take comfort in the fact that God knows what it is to struggle, what it is like to long for something, to have his body become frail and weak, some of which we felt during this process.

The Bible talks about different women unable to conceive e.g. Hannah, Sara, Rachel, Elizabeth and God intervenes, so why are we not trusting God that he will provide eventually? Or is He taking us on this journey to encourage others in the future or declare His glory in future circumstances or draw us close to Him? Rambling thoughts still pervade and there is no conclusion that even yet I have reached but I am learning to trust that God is in control and He will close this door firmly despite our human nature to knock hard on it or at times shoulder charge at it!

Would God not have given us the capability within our own bodies to have a child if it was His desire? My initial thoughts on IVF turned to cloning and Dolly the sheep but when we looked at it from a medical, logical viewpoint we saw aspects of it from a different perspective. The fact there was a clear medical reason for the fertility difficulties comforted us to pursue a medical route with God at the centre. God has created Drs with wisdom for such science.

God is the ultimate creator of life. The implantation of the embryo attaching to the womb is a miracle in itself and has to come from God as IVF cannot guarantee this or cause this to happen. We are reminded "*you knit me together* in my mother's womb" Psalm 139 13-14 and I am holding onto the belief that God will work with these little embryos and bring them to full term in circumstances where His wisdom is best. I once heard it say that the only difference between an embryo, foetus, newborn, infant and child is time. That in fact a 45 year old man/woman has everything that an embryo had This is mind blowing and opens the debate about viability of life but it comforts me to know that God has ordained life and all I can do is trust Him in the choice that we have made that He will bring it to fruition or cease it in its tracks.

Despite feeling that this was where God had us and a gradual acceptance that it was ok to go down this road, natural anxieties and doubt soon crept in. I tried to mask this emotion as excitement to try and trick my brain but at times it was overwhelming. This was compounded by the fact that during this process I had experienced stressful work environments that had at times induced panic. Why was I so anxious as a Christian, I knew God was ahead, yet my body was letting me down, no matter what my thoughts tried to override.

4

Round 1

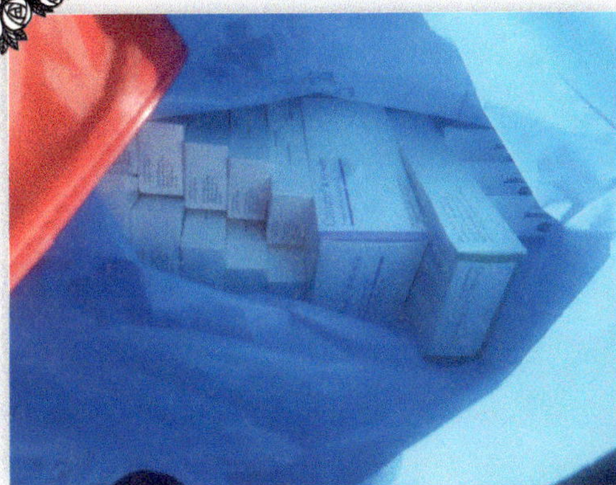

Philippians 4:13

"I can do all things through him who strengthens me."

In the red corner was a bag full of medication, some needing refrigerating, injection packs, nose sprays, tablets, a printed out protocol and some other unpleasant things necessary for this process. In the blue corner was an excited 33 year old full of hope, ready to pump this into my body, desperate to try anything if it was going to help with the desired outcome. Treatment began in February 2018 with daily nose sprays initially, described as putting my body through the menopause with all the associated symptoms. Apparently this was to have a baseline to begin intense stimulation. The aim of ICSI is to stimulate the ovaries through injection phases to produce as many follicles as possible (but not too many as this leads to overstimulation). The hope is that eggs are formed in these follicles which are then collected at a certain stage through a procedure, then fertilised with sperm outside the body and looked after by an embryologist for 1-3/5 days then transferred back if successful. Then more waiting. During the use of the twice daily nose sprays, stimulation injections were gradually introduced at different times of the day. Some creativity was required especially as these had to be administered at set times in the day so plenty were done in church or work toilet cubicles and even once in the cinema! Thankfully my sister in law is a nurse so she was able to give me a few lessons in the paraphernalia yet I still managed to cause a muscle bruise on my thigh and prick my finger a good few times. I soon became acquainted with my own personal bright yellow sharps box and a fridge shelf was taken up with medication but it would all be worth it we kept believing.

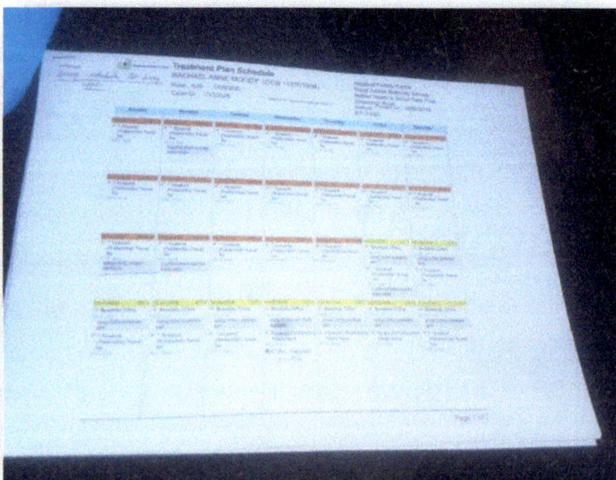

(1st treatment schedule)

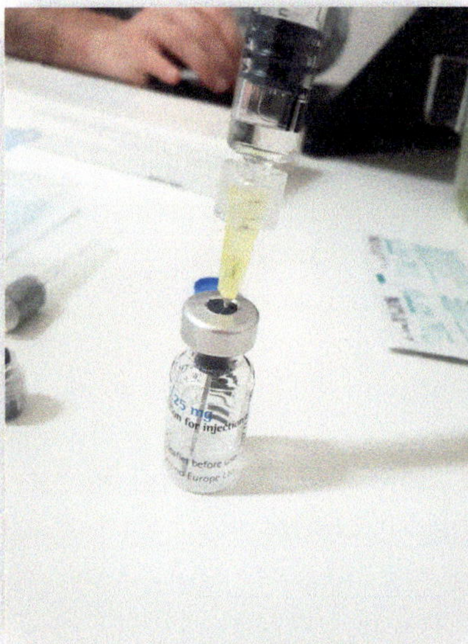

(injecting)

We threw everything at this including eating "fertility" friendly foods such as pineapple, brazil nuts, spinach and other greens. As well as trying to down at least 2 litres of water a day and trying not to go to the toilet every 5 minutes as a result. I also invested in fertility acupuncture to help with blood flow and enjoyed these sessions if anything just to give me some time out through forced relaxation. It is a very surreal feeling lying down with needles in your body and not being exactly sure what they are doing inside. Again further trust in professionals despite not understanding the process. This was a time of weight gain and feeling sorry for myself, complaining I had no clothes to wear and feeling rough with the side-effects but trying to balance this with positive thoughts of feeling blessed in so many other ways.

During March 2018 I changed jobs, hoping it would bring a better work life balance but it happened to coincide with the egg collection and scan dates a few days after I started.

Thankfully work were accommodating but it meant I had little time off to recover. Dignity was lost early on in the process. Putting your feet up in stirrups will never be glamorous and looking up at professionals with your double chin lying back is not a good look for anyone but you have to laugh about it. Egg collection (21/3/18) was an early start, fasting and a day of nerves and realisation that this was really happening, no turning back. Phil was allowed in the room which was comforting after playing his role in a classy room elsewhere. I wasn't alone, of course God was always there and already ahead in the recovery room. The morphine kicked in quickly and I began to panic as I noticed the hospital tiled roof start to spin, shouting out "the room is spinning is this ok?" - I was reassured that it was but it was an disconcerting feeling. After a few procedures and identity confirmation on the verge of sedation, the procedure was performed and I was wheeled into recovery. All of us victims that day were wheeled into the same room with a hospital curtain separating us but conversations still could be heard. I was told "Oh there are lots of Rachael's in today" which caused my half conscious mind to become paranoid thinking what if they mixed up the eggs! Irrationality was another side effect of all this which of course affected my already predisposed anxious thought pattern. When I came round a bit more I was told that 14 eggs had been collected which was a solid number so we were delighted.

(after egg collection... slightly dazed)

Armed with a pregnancy test and a few other glamorous items, I staggered back to the car after a custard cream and a glass of water. Sore and stiff, looking forward to a couple of days bed rest off work and eating a guilt free large dairy milk bar in between the water drinking regime of course which gradually my body was getting accustomed to. The days after egg collection are a strange experience. You get a set time to phone the lab to check on the progress of your precious eggs to see how fertilisation is going on a day to day basis. They grade the eggs based on the strength of survival judged by how many cells they develop into. Such a complex procedure. What a difficult job for the embryologist to communicate this news to couples on a daily basis but such important phone calls. As I was back to work I had to juggle finding a quiet place at the designated time in the toilets but thankfully God provided smooth opportunities. Our numbers looked good, out of the 14 eggs collected, 9 fertilised but then things went downhill at the last hurdle. The embryos were doing ok but not amazing. A 5 day transfer is preferred as by this stage the embryos have developed further (there is scientific language around this but I will not bore you with it) and also have the potential to begin hatching. We got an urgent call on day 3 to say we needed to come in that morning for the transfer. This was our first sign that things were not great. The two surviving embryos were transferred back and it was amazing to watch this unfold on the screen, potentially 2 little lives were now snugly back where they belonged. Despite the early transfer, I headed off to my acupuncture appointment full of hope with the idea of twins still strongly in my mind or at least "one embryo that could". From being more educated now, looking back, it was not communicated well to us anything about the quality of the embryos in language that we understood. We understand now that these little "embies" were of poor quality and not where they should have been at this stage. Another blow to deal with was that there was no additional embryos that survived so that meant there was no option for a frozen transfer on the NHS in the future and if this didn't work this time then there would be no more free opportunities. This was a shock but our priority was the two little ones inside and doing everything we could to help them stick around.

And so began the famous "2 week wait" after embryo transfer. Many report this as one of the worst stages as you have no idea or way of telling what is happening within your body. The medication can play tricks on your wellbeing and every pregnancy symptom is heightened and then googled relentlessly. We were officially PUPO (pregnant until proven otherwise). Such a difficult time, apart from advice not to do any heavy lifting, stooping or reaching, you just had to carry on as normal. For me this included being distracted by training in a new job which was a blessing as we had plenty to do and it was not stressful at all. I had met some lovely girls who I connected with so I enjoyed going into work for once. The difficulty working during this time came with feeling physically ill due to the post-transfer medication of very unpleasant progesterone. This caused numerous toilet trips so I had to vary the bathroom that I used so it didn't look like I was constantly avoiding work. The bloating was awful. I felt so stiff and uncomfortable and nothing would ease it. I struggled with the weight gain as a result of the medication. We resisted the urge to test early as you can get false positives and negatives that turn into positives etc. so we waited until nearer the test day. Your body can play tricks on you, cramping, nausea, exhaustion but you don't know if it is a result of implantation or the general effects from all the foreign chemicals you are putting into your body to help the process. Keeping busy, talking and praying during this period was our therapy.

(having acupuncture and full of hope after egg transfer)

5
Comfort in the Darkness

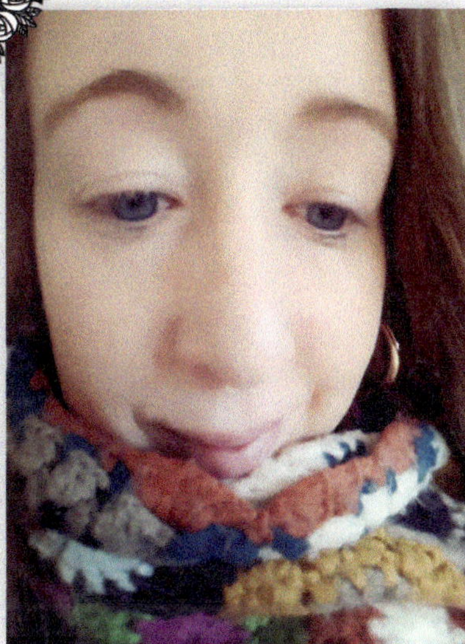

Psalm 46:1-3

"God is our refuge and strength, an ever-present help in trouble. Therefore we will not fear, though the earth give way and the mountains fall into the heart of the sea, though its waters roar and foam and the mountains quake with their surging."

By 6th April it was all over. We were due to go a wedding evening party and after getting all dressed up for one night of fun and distraction, we realised that this cycle hadn't worked for us. We drove home devastated but hoping for a miracle overnight as the official test date was not until the next morning. The pregnancy test flashed up the famous two words we had seen many times before "not pregnant". There is something quite harsh about seeing that in black and white. We both shut down a bit that day. We decided we couldn't mope about the house but rather thought about heading up to the North Coast in Northern Ireland which had become our happy place.

After a last minute booking for a hotel to treat ourselves, we made the silent drive up only to be told there had been a mix up with the booking and there was no longer a room for us. We were devastated. It seems so trivial now looking back but it was so important at the time to have a change of scenery that night. It wasn't to be and we drove home to become hermits for the rest of that weekend. I cried myself to sleep that night and many others. Phil was low and I found I was the one trying to pick him up.

The easiest option was to immediately blame God when the ground shook from beneath us but we had to remind ourselves of His promises including Jehovah-Rapha - The Lord is our healer. My realism kicked in - why should God bless us this way when actually we do very little for Him. We knew it was only a 33% chance for us yet still we were filled with so much hope.

A few weeks earlier in church, Phil had been comforted by a verse promising hope "the following Spring" and had held onto such hope that this was our season of Spring literally but it wasn't to be which caused confusion as we felt certain for success. Darkness is lonely, isolating and in the case of a failed IVF cycle, it is a silent place. No one calls round with homemade meals or you aren't overwhelmed with messages and calls as not many people know of your journey and those that do, it can be awkward for them and they want to give you space. Yet, in the darkness, you are catapulted closer to God, which is far greater than any loss you can experience. Was it a miscarriage since it was very early on? No matter what it was, it felt like two losses of potential live for us. God reminds us He will collect our tears and the Holy Spirit surrounded us in this time and brought us through many rivers of tears. Perhaps we were too hopeful for this first time around which made the fall all the more difficult. A few months later we had a review appointment at which we were very briefly just told "it was the luck of the dice" However, we knew God had us in His hands no matter what the outcome and had ordained this day before we were both even born.

Over the years of stressful work circumstances, I became a professional at putting on a mask in public despite crumbling inside. That time had come again. Normal duties were resumed. A mask of normality was worn among friends that were unaware as well as in work and church environments. I didn't mind talking about it and sharing the journey but I had to respect Phil's privacy.

Loneliness lingered no matter how much I cried out to God yet I still sensed He had got this. There is a saying in the IVF community "IVF got this" but I always knew I had a God bigger than IVF, bigger than fertility issues as "God's got this" and He provided the comfort needed in this dark season. Worship music became my comfort on days when the Bible was just too hard to read.

Music can be so encouraging, relevant and uplifting in so many of our life circumstances and this brought much peace. Lots of favourites are named on the back pages. I hope you are encouraged. They still hold so much meaning for myself today on good and bad days. Despite the tears, hope and peace became the overriding emotions. Only God could instil that and transform the human emotion of a negative situation.

Psalm 121 has always had significant meaning for us. It was preached on at our wedding, I read it at my brother's wedding and it was a favourite of my parents which took on extra meaning after my dad died suddenly in 2010. *"I lift up my eyes to the hills-- where does my help come from? My help comes from the LORD, the Maker of heaven and earth."* We continued to lift our eyes to the mountains which seemed mighty to be moved yet we believe God is able. Like the pain being experienced, Jesus also felt pain, far greater than any suffering we have or will face. Yet still He gave glory to God. Jesus is the only light and hope in any of our darkest circumstances and seasons.

We spent the next few months debating what to do next. We always thought we would try privately as we thought the treatment would be better and more advanced in relation to our medical condition but finances held us back. We decided to take the summer as a breather as we had a family holiday coming up and knew treatment schedules would impact this. After the summer we received a sum of money as inheritance from my Grandparents which was real blessing, a special legacy and very timely to cover another round of IVF.

We took this as an open sign to try privately but how can we be sure this was from God? This is what we continue to struggle with to a degree. After our failed first cycle, we had a very welcomed visit from our pastor who had heard of our situation from a family member. He made us feel very comfortable with our decision to pursue this IVF route which gave us comfort to keep travelling this road for now.

We wanted to do something to remember the little embryos that didn't survive so we planted a cherry blossom tree to remember that life goes on and there can still be seasons of bloom.

(recovery)

6

Round 2

Luke 1:37

"For nothing will be impossible with God."

This time in the blue corner was two private NI fertility clinics and in the red corner a couple who were excited to start another adventure but clueless of what to do as we were totally on our own now out of the system. I went to an open evening for one clinic, Phil was unable to go at the last minute. This proved to be an awkward evening whenever I asked a question, it was presumed because I was there on my own, that I was seeking a sperm donor. It seems common enough in the IVF community!

We did some research and knew that in Northern Ireland there wouldn't be much done differently the next time for us. Due to the specific medical condition that was our situation, we found out that by going abroad for treatment, this could provide better medical advances and strangely at a lesser cost. Obviously many factors needed to be weighed up as we would be away from home for potentially 8/10 days in a foreign country, away from our support network and not knowing the language.

Prague was determined to be the most advanced in the area that we required so after a few emails to some clinics there, we settled on Gynem in Prague. We had a free Skype consultation and felt comfortable to proceed. Having a coordinator speaking English was amazing so that barrier was gone immediately. After some scans at home and a delivery of medication for the fridge again, we were good to start the famous injections. The stomach bloating and weight gain would commence with full force this time. The downside with going away for treatment is the lack of organisation that is out of your control e.g. booking flights, accommodation, dates to be off work.

It all depends on your body responding to medication, results of scans and the timing of this. Both of our workplaces were thankfully supportive and flexible. It is an awkward conversation to have with a younger male line manager that you are going through this intimate process but he was flexible in knowing that I may not have exact dates until a few days before. Phil's boss was extremely supportive and he was allowed to work for a few days over in Prague remotely which was a massive help.

(medication from Prague delivery)

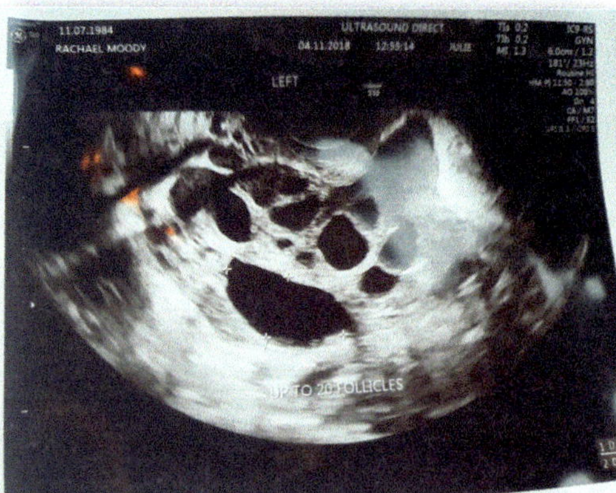

(one of many follicle scans)

So off we went to Prague for a "holiday". We did not tell as many people this time around as we thought maybe that this would take the pressure off. We were both full of hope and excitement more so this time as we half knew what to expect in the process so we were more relaxed. The day after we arrived we went to the clinic. Thankfully they had arranged transfers there which made the whole process much smoother. It was a strange feeling walking into a foreign setting and not knowing what many of the staff were saying in the background but all the way we were leaning on God and carried a sense of excitement.

That appointment was not what we were expecting. All of a sudden things crumbled a bit. After another undignified scan I was told that I had far too many follicles and there was too much stimulation so I was now over stimulated. This meant I had developed something called OHSS: Ovarian hyper stimulation syndrome. I was told by the consultant who seemed harsh, half translated through my English coordinator, that we would not be able to complete the process at this time as it would be too dangerous for my health and that my body would not be able to sustain a pregnancy right now as I needed additional medication to calm down the follicle growth.

I was told that we would delay the egg collection while they tried to get things calmed down for the rest of the week and then they would have to halt the process with a freeze all cycle ending. This was gutting as last time we had nothing survive to the day 5 for freezing so we were naturally concerned that this would be the case again.

(off to Gynem)

The main thing about the clinic abroad that was negative was that Phil was not allowed in the room for any scans or procedures. I'm sure that this was difficult for him as he often felt removed from the process. This meant when I came out from this room and told Phil, I couldn't slow the tears.

Therefore I appeared to the staff there to be some hormonal crier when in reality my mind had just flashed back to the feelings of the last failure. We realised we were not going to be home as quickly as we thought and ended up having to book new accommodation every other day as it wasn't clear how long this would take. One thing was clear, we would be returning to Northern Ireland without any little embryos inside, but if we were fortunate enough, they would remain in a Czech freezer until we could return. Over the next week we laid low on the days when I was feeling rough and tried to see some of the sights on the better days. After checking in at the clinic during the week we finally got a date for the egg collection. I felt like a whale. My trousers would not button and I was so glad I had packed a few 'floaty' dresses which I lived in. My stomach had swollen up like I was pregnant, an unfortunate side effect of the OHSS. I was so sore and stiff still for many weeks afterwards.

For egg collection (12/11/18) I was presented with a delightful Eastern European green stripey nightdress and a pair of freshly laundered white trainer socks. I was just glad I wasn't given the second option reserved for the next girl, a faded pink nighty with "I am purrfect" on it in the image of a big cat which was creepy in itself. It was a daunting experience as I waited in a bay cubicle with other anxious women in similar situations around me. It was an early start but better to get it over with.

I was injected with anaesthetic and watched the famous hospital ceiling tiles start to swirl again but this time I was knocked out completely. I woke up groggy in the initial hospital bay after what I thought was ten minutes later but turns out it was a few hours. I was just thankful that I had woken up at all! I was told they managed to get 26 eggs so we were told "the extra stimulation was worth it". Perhaps that was the case but my body was saying no more!

I also started to panic thinking if all these embryos became viable in the coming days, how could we move forward with this ethical nightmare but knew God had it and would bring to fruition what His plan was. Unbeknown to me, Phil was upstairs waiting and in a scary conversation himself. The coordinator had come to him and asked him to step outside of the waiting room and sit down - he would later say that he thought something serious had happened to me during the procedure. In actual fact he was being told that there had been a multidisciplinary meeting that morning with the head of the clinic about me as I had so many follicles and what the best course of treatment was after egg collection, whether they would definitely freeze all as had been recommended. Turns out this recommendation remained so there was no change to the plan. The next day or so was a blur as we stayed in the hotel room, watching Netflix downloads and scoffing our way through a 20 piece chicken nugget meal that evening. But we were together and this forced time of rest was refreshing.

(big McNugget's meal)

The next stage was the anxious wait for the email from our coordinator - a day by day account of how the egg and sperm were getting on. We didn't make it past day 3 last time so the wait was worrying. The email came at different times during the day so I became a bit obsessive refreshing the page hoping for positive written words. Up until day 2 the numbers were looking well then as before, they quickly diminished. They talk about the embryo quality in terms of grading and cell numbers and by day 2 we had rapidly reduced down to

3 embryos which were looking good for freezing in 3 days time. Day 3 was the last day in Prague for us so we went to the cinema that night to see 'A Star is born'. The email had not come through during the day so this was concerning in itself. The film was emotional enough never mind the fact that I had checked my phone during it to see an email of concern from Hana our coordinator.

Overnight, the picture was now much bleaker. As I broke the news to Phil, we managed to find a sofa outside the cinema toilets to process the email while eating the remains of the savoury cheesy popcorn (an order lost in translation) and trying to hide glum faces. Hana had mentioned that the embryos had now become "very fragmented" and quality was "worsening". She went on to put in black and white "the cells of each of you do not fit/match each other and it may be worth considering donor's cells".

This statement will stay with me. It was harsh to read it. They were saying that this process wasn't working for us like before because we were not a match together. This made me question everything in a flash on that Czech sofa, our choice to go down the IVF road, questioning God. Phil sent a few prayer request texts to his friends as we felt desperate that we were losing it all again after such high hopes. After being more rational over time about the situation we were still so blessed in abundant ways and who are we to question anything that God gives or takes away. Anything additional is a blessing.

The next day a miracle happened. After the egg quality regressing, suddenly it progressed more so than before which I never thought would be possible. We were told that we now had 4 suitable for freezing (2 at a time on the one 'straw'). Getting this news as we got off the plane in Belfast was perfect timing and hope was restored. This was confirmed the next day when 2 good quality and 2 average quality embryos had survived the 5 days. We were so grateful.

In the end, we spent 2 weeks in Prague. A lovely city for a 3 day break but we knew it well after our lengthy stay. Prague was full of adventure including exploring the transport links, getting escorted to the nearest ATM to pay a fine by the Prague transport police, trying to find free public toilets, finding the closest McDonalds and comfort eating till we burst (I didn't have much room in my stomach area after the OHSS). No matter what it will always be a special place for us. Each night during that time, I decided to do some Bible journaling. This creative outlet helped me focus my thoughts on the bigger picture and to not be consumed by this human frailty that was before us but rather to keep looking up and focussed above.

(Beautiful Prague)

Coming home was a bit of an anti climax as we thought we would have been on the pregnancy journey but rather we came home with a pregnant shaped belly but with nothing inside. The bloating and stiffness continued but we knew as in every circumstance that hope was ahead and that kept us going. We had such busy lives before and I had never really felt ill but now my body was telling me to slow down and I began to say no to different social engagements to give my body time to recover as we had 4 little frosties that were waiting for us and we wanted to reach them as soon as we could.

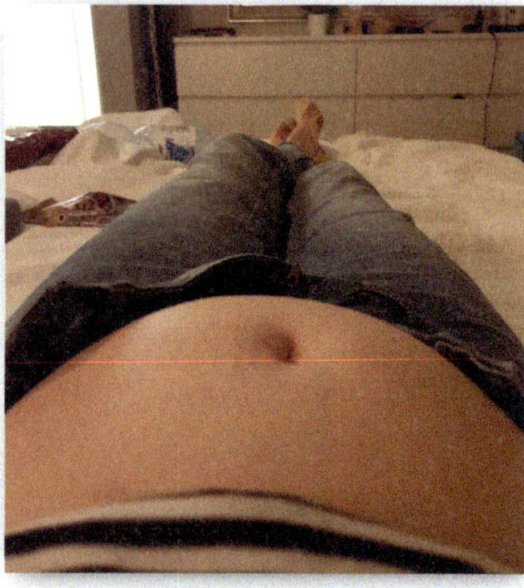

(OHSS effects)

(little embryos on video)

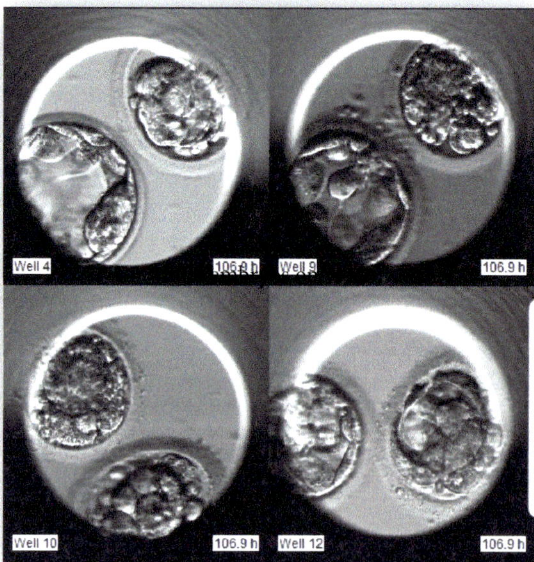

7

Christmas 2018

Isaiah 9 v 6

"For to us a child is born, to us a son is given, and the government will be on his shoulders. And he will be called Wonderful Counselor, Mighty God, Everlasting Father, Prince of Peace."

Christmas Eve would have been our due date we had worked out from our first round of failed IVF in March. This was always in the back of my mind. Saying good bye to another year where your plans didn't come to fruition in any circumstance is hard but a new year also brings great expectancy. By this stage, I was starting to fit back into my old jeans slightly, at times with a long top and the button undone but it was better than not at all. Work (now in a new environment) remained busy but at least the day flew by.

I was really missing my jogging and exercising but I was trying to let my body recover while eating as best as I could. Ideally we should have went back to Prague in December but with Christmas, the clinic was closed for a couple of weeks so it was not meant to be. January it was then. But we learnt over Christmas that I needed to have another scan at home before they could send the medication for the frozen embryo transfer. Of course due to the Christmas timing, this was unable to be done until January so this pushed on our return date to the middle of February ('ish').

Everything is always "ish" in the IVF world as things can change in a matter of days. Christmas can be a tough time for many people. For some reason, I found this one tougher than most years. Perhaps subconsciously I was thinking of the little embryos that didn't make it in March or dealing with the emotion of Novembers experience or more likely the impact of all that medication that tends to linger in your system.

Phil and I both just felt frustrated about the ongoing circumstances out of our control and took this wrongly out on each other. We had drifted from God and couldn't remember the last time we had prayed together. My body felt like it had taken a battering yet what I had went through was nothing compared to anyone living with any kind of illness so I had no right to complain. Christmas Eve was a low point, we both felt physically and mentally drained. Minor things can turn into arguments and patience can be in short supply when frustration feelings overwhelm during the IVF journey. Sometimes we just had to shake ourselves out of a rut, whether it was going for a walk or having a cry and getting on with something. Or as the case on Christmas eve, watching 'Meet me in St Louis' with a cup of hot chocolate and trying to switch off and remember the real reason for the season ahead.

We are so so blessed and thankful to have so many children in our lives from cousins children to friends children and our special nephews Ellis and recent addition Lucas. It can sting at times when you are the only person in a situation without children or when you are helping in crèche at church yet feel inadequate but we need to remind ourselves that we can have purpose without being a parent, this does not and should not define who we are even though the world can imply so. I was so conscious not to let it consume me as it could easily. Private scans aren't cheap especially around December/January time when there is so much to pay out.

The scan place in Belfast was very sensitive to the circumstance and the girl was so lovely. However, it is hard going to a place known for baby scans and yet your scan option is the one in fine print on the leaflet. Sitting in a waiting room with bumps around you is tough never mind hearing excitement and raised voices coming from the next room where a gender scan was taking place "you are going to have a boy!". You have to be happy for other people. I never wanted to turn into the bitter IVF woman who detested all babies and made things uncomfortable for family and friends going through pregnancy. Yes it can be hard but that could be you one day in the midst of baby bliss and they deserve that moment. When I hear a pregnancy announcement I try to make a point of praying for the mum and baby right there which really helps any bitterness or jealousy that was to creep in. By doing something practical like that it can serve to bring peace.

The waiting continued and just after Christmas, the medication arrived for the frozen embryo transfer. I purchased one of those tablet boxes for morning, noon and night that my auntie used to prepare for my Granda every Sunday. I had become organised if nothing else. Twelve tablets daily was going to be rough. On some days I would have gladly swapped them for the injections. It was strange knowing that 4 embryos that were ours remained in another country. Part of us was miles away, yet we were closer than before to hopefully meeting some if not all of them in the future.

But again Isaiah 43 v 19 was a timely reminder at Christmas time going into the new year "I *will make a way* in the wilderness and rivers in the desert."

8
Round 2.5

2 Corinthians 12:9

"My grace is sufficient for you, for my power is made perfect in weakness."

Ding ding ding here we went again. Round 2 and a half although it felt like a full 3rd round of ICSI as I undertook new medication, scans and procedures. In the blue corner was the foreign medication in the corner of the bedroom tucked into a Nike shoe box and in the red corner, a couple trusting they had chosen the right path, anxious to return to that lab in the Czech republic which held precious cargo. After further scans at home, we were given the go ahead to travel over a few days later for the frozen embryo transfer on 13/2/19. Travel this time around was a bit more complicated. There was no direct flights from Belfast on the specific days that we needed to travel so we had to have a stopover for a long afternoon in London there and back. Compared to very cheap flights last time, this time the total came to about £500 but again no obstacle seemed too large.

We decided to stay in a central hotel to make things run smoothly. We had the most amazing breakfast on the day of embryo transfer until we realised that it was not included in the overnight stay. But it was worth it, the babies would need some sustenance that day and a salted caramel extra large muffin was a great way to start! We hadn't heard anything from the clinic that morning so thought no news is good news and things must be moving as planned. The big thaw was planned for the morning and we had to arrive at 12.30 for the paperwork and the main event. After a familiar tram journey to the clinic, we were told that the 2 embryos had thawed well and their quality was not impacted at all!

Get them in my belly was all I was thinking. After confirming my details with the embryologist through a tiny lab window, the correct embryos were selected as I lay back in the familiar room. I often wondered what if they mix up the embryos or things get confused but science is so mind-blowing these days that everything is highly coded and access is prevented unless specific ID and codes are confirmed. Thankfully there was no night dress to wear this time, just a lovely half see through white tutu for the glamorous occasion and the old familiar white trainer socks which seem to be popular in Prague but for me not so much.

I was awake the whole time which was lovely as I got to see 2 potential little lives again on the screen find their way into their potential new home. They looked so round and perfect, a mix of Phil and I in there somewhere, who knows what they could become. I was delighted at the prospect of a potential multiple birth. I was officially 'PUPO' by an Eastern European catheter. The whole experience was and remains very surreal. Later that day we went to Phil's happy place, a huge shopping mall in Prague where we did some retail therapy before going back to rest at the hotel. For the transfer, they recommend no heavy lifting, straining etc. afterwards during the 2 week wait but you are encouraged to return to work and to walk around to stimulate the blood flow. I am not one for sitting around anyway but I became suddenly conscious of every twinge or lift I was doing.

Phil was great, always pre-empting if I forgot myself for a minute and when we got home, his mum wasn't going to let him forget anyway. The next day was Valentine's day and we were on the commute home. The official day of love and we could not have any more love for these little cells inside of me yet to implant. Such a flying visit this time so much so that many didn't know we were away. Again having the week off work was the best decision as I could relax at home, knowing I was giving this my best shot. I only did things that made me happy including seeing friends and family and had to say no to a few commitments (which is not in my nature) but knew it would only be temporary. Armed with further medication to aid the process, the familiar 2 week wait began.

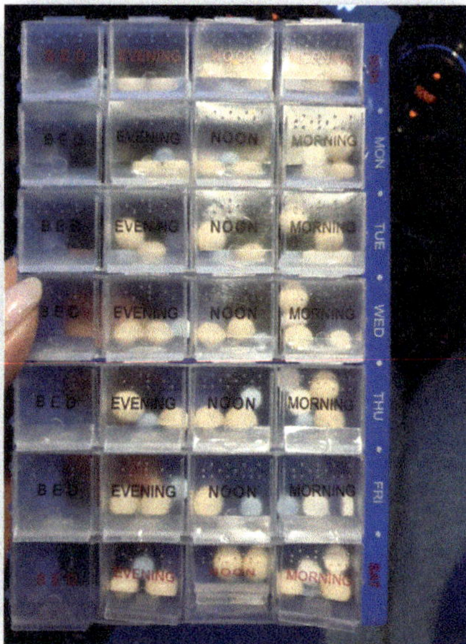

(some of the daily intake)

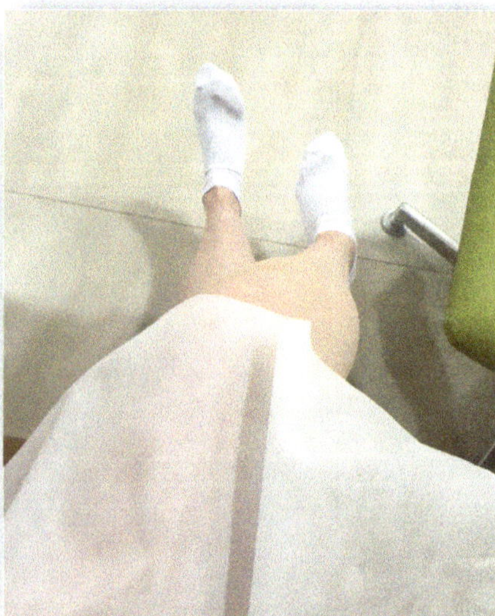

(Tutu love)

9
Aftermath

Romans 12v12

"Be joyful in hope, patient in affliction, faithful in prayer."

I can honestly say that this round took the worst toll on my body. Aside from the OHSS last time, it was the medication this time that caused me the most side effects. Since the transfer I had been drained of all energy. Specific progesterone style tablets had caused me lots of drowsiness and dizziness. At one stage Phil had to almost catch me as my legs buckled a bit with the drowsiness. Phil drove lots during this time! The 12 tablets continued and we were told that they would have to be taken for 3 months if this was a successful pregnancy. I struggled with being so bloated as it caused plenty of weight gain. At least if I was pregnant that would be acceptable but at this early stage, the face weight in particular frustrated me. I felt powerless to do anything about it as no significant high impact exercise was allowed but I did a few walks around the block to keep my sanity.

Conflicting voices told me I should be at work while others told me I needed to take some time off. I knew my body and knew it wasn't right but as much as I struggled with work at present, I believed that the day would go in quickly and it would transport me somewhere else other than my thoughts on 'will this work?'. Work is a strange place to experience IVF. Obviously women become pregnant, naturally ladies talk about their children and grandchildren and you have nothing to add to that conversation. It's a fine line between people knowing and then feeling uncomfortable talking around you or knowing and being supportive. I didn't mind who knew but it was not something that I advertised either. It is isolating in the workplace nonetheless. Trying to chose the right time to inject/medicate that won't have the most adverse effects or your thoughts secretly consuming you inside or your ability to focus but you have to answer the phone and deal with the public and whatever is thrown your way on days when the situation feels heavy.

Juggling the hospital scan appointments can be tricky too, although you should be entitled to them it is awkward asking sometimes no later than a week of each other to get another afternoon off, never mind trying to explain to observant colleagues what for.

Every cramp, twinge and back ache filled me with hope that things might be progressing inside but then negativity crept in thinking it could be a range of other things. I tried to eat healthier during this time, cutting out fizzy drinks, downing many litres of water, adding more spinach to recipes, eating the healthy freezer meals I had prepared before we went and drinking more green fruit and vegetable smoothies. However there were plenty of days during that 2 week wait that I craved sugar, ate a family sized bag of crisps, a cheese board, a few crème eggs in a row or a salted caramel galaxy bar convincing myself the "babies" wanted it or I deserved a treat after feeling rotten while being on the medication.

I had never felt tiredness like it but hope remained and we tried to carry on as normal. My body felt old beyond its years and I was looking forward to reclaiming it back from all the chemicals I was putting into it. I had some lazy days watching Lifetime movies on YouTube or box sets of Jonathan Creek or Silent Witness which was my escapism from reality and they did their job well.

I caved in and tested on our 4 year anniversary (one week after transfer). This test was faintly positive but we pushed this out of our mind as we knew nothing would be confirmed until a potential early scan but oh what hope and joy it gave us. We went away that weekend so it was lovely to be by ourselves and have some proper rest, a good distraction from the inquiries of others and from us getting too anxious about the whole situation.

Then 27th February 2019 arrived. Official test day ("OTD"). Another pregnancy test purchased and a few more in different brands just to be extra sure. I wanted the one that had it in writing. PREGNANT there is was, how ridiculously shocked, amazed and thankful we were. Now what to do, after waiting for this moment, we didn't know what to do with it. It didn't seem real and still doesn't. I contacted the early pregnancy clinic to see if we could easily slot into the system as we had been away for treatment and how this would work but thankfully I just fitted into the world of a typical pregnant woman from then on A world I honestly never imagined I would ever get a glimpse into. No matter what was to happen, we were blessed to have seen two lines on a positive pregnancy test and the official words in black and white staring back at us. Even if it never happens again, we will never forget that feeling.

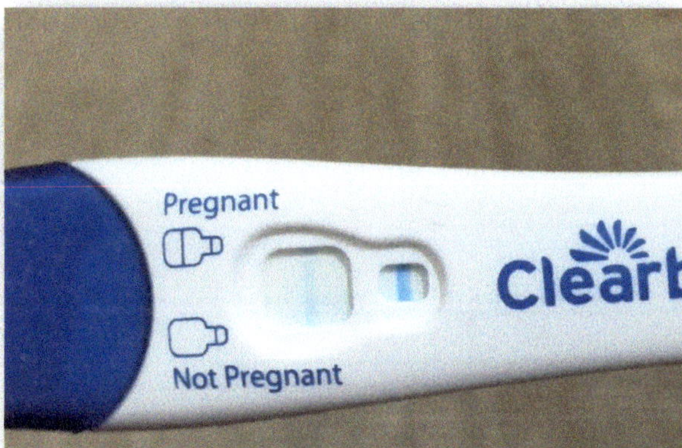

(a good day)

10
Emotion Overload

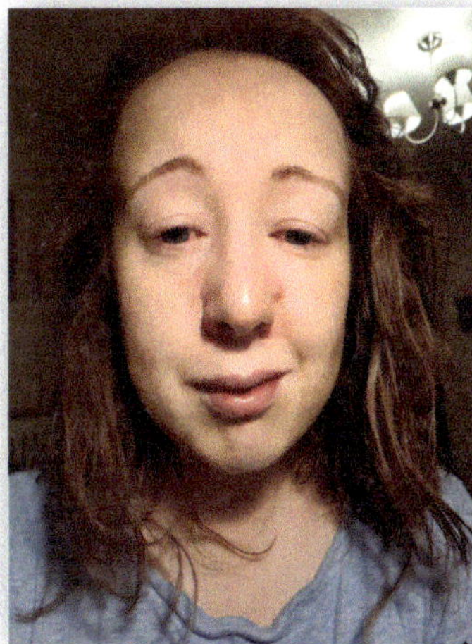

Isaiah 41 v 10

"Do not fear for I am with you"

Throughout this whole journey, fear and anxiety could have easily been a forerunner. I'll be honest and say they were high on the list but HOPE was the overarching emotion and won over darkness. Nevertheless they are and remain very real in many situations for many people. Anxiety has overwhelmed my soul in relation to my work choices and environment. I have felt lost there and still at 36 remain unsure of my occupational path. Every day I struggle with this workplace anxiety but busyness keeps my thoughts occupied. Anxiety in relation to ICSI for me was not necessarily that it wasn't going to work but that if it didn't, maybe we wouldn't pass an adoption or fostering process and then we would have no option to have children in our home. Always thinking one step ahead is not always good. My anxiety was not centred as much on not having children biologically of my own (although this was and remains a strong desire) but that we could never have children to love in our own home or caring for any child long-term.

Worship music on a loop was my helper and calmer in times of creeping fear and anxious thoughts. There was fear in the form of spending so much money on this process that could have went to other things that we practically needed or savings. But we reminded ourselves that this could be supporting little lives to grow into men or women of faith and who knows with God's help what they could achieve in the future.

A strange fear came over me at times also which will seem ridiculous. What if it does work? All we had known so far on this journey was failure and had been consumed by that. If it did work, would we be capable of doing this? Would we be able to do this next very much wanted stage of the journey? Again all irrational but by this stage the hormones had exploded. The reality is that in every situation, God is ahead, standing in the midst of the outcome, there is nothing we can do to change it. He is already there waiting with arms wider than the situation being faced. The tough job is reassuring the brain of this fact and in turn passing the message onto the body. Despite worry being a natural response to many dark times that we face and valleys that we will walk through, God is with us. I still feel guilty worrying when I know this fact and believe it with all my heart.

Guilt has also been along with us for the ride and remains a familiar friend to both of us. We both have individual guilt for separate reasons why we are on this assisted reproductive journey in the first place. Phil has felt guilty that he has not had to do much practically on this journey and naturally as a man in this process, he does not bear the brunt of using medication, yet I could not have got through it without him. We have felt guilty for feeling down or depressed about our circumstance when there are so many other people in our land and world in much worse off situations. We know of friends and family members who are single and their hearts desire is to be with someone and we are so blessed to have each other. Friends throughout this process have been facing their own struggles, dealing with cancer and suicide in their families or facing storms we could not imagine. Yet I found myself crying over not being able to have a baby at this time.

I have felt guilt in the waiting as continually see advertisements for organisations desperate for foster carers or hearing someone in church talk about their fostering journey. My heart aches knowing that we have 2 bedrooms in our house that could be used for these desperate situations yet we can't do anything until we see this process out. This conflict still remains in my heart. I have felt guilty at others showing us undeserved support far beyond measure at times. When I was ill the first time in Prague, I got a text message from my cousin telling us she was fasting for us and praying for us that specific day. This just blew my mind why people would feel this burden for us.

At an event in church where an adoption/fostering story was being shared another lovely friend approached me at the end as she felt I was placed on her heart. Again I did not feel worthy for such attention when so many are suffering so much greater. My mum has found it difficult without my dad around to have that support to talk to many people about the situation. I had felt so guilty for not giving her the opportunity to be a grandparent yet as I know this would be her heart's desire also or my brother for him not becoming an uncle yet. The same emotion is felt for my all of my grandparents who have all passed away in the past few years. O how I would have longed for them to meet any future child of ours as they had such an influence in my life. I know Phil would feel the same about his grandparents. My mum confided in her hairdresser and friend about our situation and she put a prayer for us in the wailing wall in Jerusalem while on a recent trip to the Holy Lands. Again an overwhelming thing to have done for us. I have spent many hours researching online or on the infertility forums where that time could have been spent reading the Bible. I will always remember that I owe God so much of my life and time yet the reality is I give Him very little, so why should we expect any of His blessings. Our pastor has been very supportive and taken an interest in asking us about our journey, but even this interest we feel we are not worthy of it as within such a large church there are so many greater needs.

My initial feeling of guilt was around the idea of "paying for a baby" but we were able to resolve this by focusing on the medical treatment aspect which was what we were paying for. The most recent feeling of guilt has centred around these frozen embryos. Perhaps we naively did not research fully this whole process, blinded by the desire to have a baby. I understand there are at least a million "snowflake babies" abandoned in freezers in so many IVF clinics around the world. This is decades of frozen embryos waiting for adoptive parents.

Even though we are well along in this journey, this has caused me unease recently. This idea of suspending life. In reality, our little Prague embryos were all conceived as such in November 2018, yet half of them brought closer to fulfilling their potential in February 2019 while the other 2 remained for the next round. What happens if I develop cancer or there is the death of one us, those little embryos remain. We all do not know what a day can bring. This fills me with some shame, surely this is not how God intended but all I can do is reconcile this with God, pray, ask for His forgiveness in all things and surrender the situation to Him. This has brought me some peace knowing that in all things we have a Saviour who is greater than these earthly conflicts and human thoughts. Like the polar bear trapped in the Prague zoo, emotions are relentless and often circular, to-ing and fro-ing until there is a better outcome.

11
Family and Friends

1 Thessalonians 5:11

"Therefore encourage one another and build one another up."

We have been blessed by the support of family and friends during this process. This has ranged from special friends sending an encouraging text message, a phone call, a bottle of Schloer and a chocolate muffin left on the doorstep on a rainy day, surprise flowers from another or a funny meme or reminder of a childhood movie sent by my brother to make me smile . My mum did and still does send consistent thoughtful cards through the post which have always been a source of encouragement. I will always cherish the influence of both my loving parents and their nurture towards my brother and I despite whatever they were facing. It has left a legacy that I hope to follow. My mother in law offered lots of practical support including offering to do the washing and ironing whenever we were away. Phil loves this as I refuse to iron his underwear, socks and other items that don't need ironed unlike his mum, so he gets this luxury back again.

The majority of our close friends all have children or are expecting as I write this. We have went through many pregnancy announcements since we got married. We are delighted for all of our friends but naturally it can be difficult emotionally. There was one year where 3 of my closest friends and sister in law all had children that same year so at times I became paranoid thinking they would now distance themselves from me because I was not in the mum club but thankfully that wasn't to be but the mind can play tricks. At a child's birthday party one year another adult there asked me "where's yours?" as all of my friends had their children there and I was there on my own.

I was able to brush this off but the comment stabbed deep and yet there was no malice in it. I was just so sensitive at the time. Thankfully an amazing friend noticed and supported me through that ground swallowing moment. However, we love seeing them and feel honoured that we get to be involved in their little lives already and hopefully watch them grow up. Our nephews makes us smile every time we see them and bring the whole family so much joy.

Family members all have opinions too. We are known for having busy lives but during times of treatment they tended to voice that we were doing too much or running around too much. I had a different perspective. We were doing things that brought us joy, catching up with friends, going to events, it was all things that became therapeutic rather than distressing so we continued to make our own choices. People began to assert their influence over when I should be returning to work. I did not want them to turn around and say if it didn't work that it was because I went back to work too soon. This would be unfair. I decided to compromise and take a few days off but it was encouraged to return to work but just not to do anything too physical. As much as I didn't want to go back, I knew I would need future time off and didn't want a sick record this early on in the year.

It is an embarrassing thing, knowing that your family especially and friends know about an intimate detail of your life. No one else would be telling their family this early on if they were pregnant or not or exactly when the egg and sperm have been fertilised. I don't mind talking about my experience but I did not want every detail known yet lots of questions were asked. We just wanted some privacy at the time so I struggled with this aspect when questions were asked about what exactly a procedure involved or what exactly did the lab say. I am happy to talk about it now but it was emotional in the midst of it all. We tried to keep things general to manage their expectations also and we were grateful that they cared.

Many times we were told by random people we came in contact with "you need to catch up" or asked "are you not thinking of kids?". I don't think I would ever think to ask this of someone I knew or not and we are both so much more sensitive to the issue now naturally in relation to other people. My response was usually "it is in the plan but it just hasn't happened yet". I wanted to voice to people that we did actually want kids but we were having trouble getting to that destination. Phil tended to respond with "oh we have so much to do in the house still" but this made me mad. At times I felt like saying we were on an IVF treatment plan but I had to reign myself in as I was conscious not to make other people feel uncomfortable.

Plenty will also say "maybe if you don't think about it too much it can happen" but this isn't always the case and it can be hard to switch off from something all consuming. Another unhelpful comment can be "I'm sure it might happen if you relax". In our situation this was not an obvious factor as there was a medical reason so no one knows what is going on in the background, but I appreciate people are just trying to help. If you know anyone going through fertility treatment or experiencing difficulties in this area and don't know what to say, do something practical. Send them a text message letting them know you are thinking of them, send them an encouraging verse or song, post them a care package or a doorstep delivery of treats, take them out for brunch, go for a walk or do some fun happy activity together. It will be so appreciated as the silence of fertility difficulties can be a difficult challenge.

Another thing about fertility treatment is that you are robbed of surprising others with your pregnancy news. You end up explaining the process and I did not mind that but then it means that people know early on if the treatment has not worked or is looking like it may be a viable pregnancy. Because there was no element of surprise we were able to change our scan date and took back some element of control and surprise. This meant we could announce our pregnancy once it was confirmed at the early pregnancy clinic to our families slightly sooner than they expected as they had a different date for the appointment in mind. Although this was earlier in the process than a typical pregnancy, it was still nice to have a moment of control.

Naturally, everyone was overjoyed for us and close cousins even shed tears which was extremely touching. It felt like many friends and family were on this journey with us. My sister in laws sent encouraging messages and gave practical support such as bags of treats to help with morning sickness on the doorstep.

My close friends were also so supportive through prayer and encouragement. It was amazing to find out that one of my bridesmaids was also having a baby due two weeks before us so it was so lovely to be on the pregnancy journey with her. It turned out a few girls in church and other friends were due in the same year so this affirmed that God's timing was apparent as I have had such a lovely community of close friends who have given me so much wisdom who have had babies at similar stages or have slightly older children who have given me so much helpful advice.

The further we got through the pregnancy, the more people we felt we could tell and it became apparent that many had been thinking of us in the background, we felt very unworthy as who were we when people have such challenges behind closed doors in their own lives. A friend whose daughter also went through IVF announced it to her knitting club and she has given me some beautiful knitted items which I will treasure.

While another friend's mum prayed for us on her prayer list and even my close friends in laws were holding us up in prayer along with some people in their church so were rejoicing with us. I will never forget the support. Upon telling one of my aunt and uncle's the good news, they were elated and told us that they had prayed for us daily which really humbled us both. My Nanny also expressed the news as an answer to prayer. They are all such a faithful servants of God so we were really touched by their daily prayers when the world is full of so much else to be worthy of prayer and praise.

Naturally I'm guessing many friends and perhaps family had opinions on going through IVF as a Christian but I'm glad that they stayed silent on the issue as I don't know if my thoughts could have coped with any further conflict. Though now I am further on in this journey I would value their wisdom and honesty. At the time I did not want anyone to say we shouldn't do it as we knew that was likely our only option humanly speaking but God is greater and we must not forget that. I would love further Christian opinions on the controversial topic as this aspect I still struggle with and find reading material hard to come by.

(Sarah Cameron Art)

12
The following Spring

Psalm 30 v 5

"Weeping may tarry for the night, but joy comes with the morning"

Pregnancy was my spring and joy. It was Good Friday when we had our 3 month scan and this was another assurance on the day that Jesus gave His life for us, I was seeing a little life that he died for to save on a screen. We had been to the early pregnancy clinic to determine if the pregnancy was viable or not at 7 weeks, as often the hormone change may have been a chemical pregnancy or false/positive etc. The heartbeat sound never failed to send tingles down your spine. As this book is focussed on the IVF journey, I don't want to go into every detail about the pregnancy or dwell on it as I still feel for so many women who are yearning for this experience. However I will touch on a few points as throughout it we felt so blessed and sustained by God.

I loved being pregnant and experiencing having a bump although physically I felt so unwell. For the first 3 months I continued to take around 10 tablets daily to help sustain the pregnancy and I think the medication had a big part to play in the nausea. However, the sickness lasted until about 24 weeks then returned again towards the end but I knew it would all be worth it. The constant sickness and relentless lack of energy levels was challenging, especially commuting and having full days in work but I felt guilty ever talking about it or complaining as so many longed to be in my position and would go through anything to be there. I have never ate so many Subway sandwiches, prawn cocktail crisps and savoury snacks during those 9 months. Ginger, peppermint oil, anti-sickness bands and many other remedies were tried but what helped most was the honesty of some women who had been there before. They stated that the sickness may last the whole time and it just has to pass which it will and this actually helped me to accept it more and lower my expectations for it ending.

I felt guilty cancelling plans I had made to meet up with people but eventually realised that this was now time to slow down if ever there was one. The busyness of life can only be maintained for a season. Jesus spoke to the Apostles in Mark 6v31 and said "Come away by yourselves to a desolate place and rest a while." No matter what circumstances we run into, it is important to walk to a place of rest.

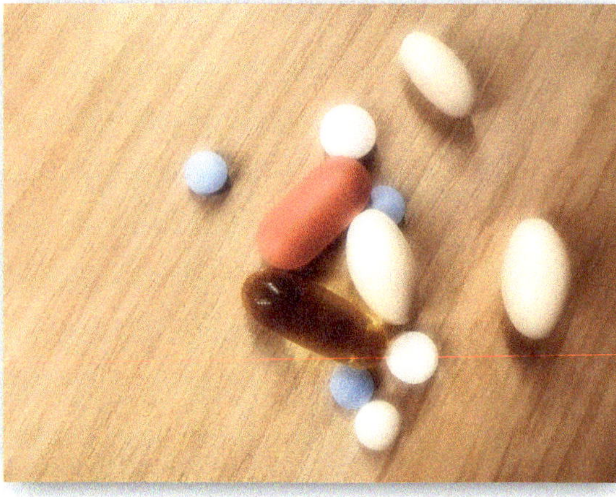

(daily concoctions)

At times it was overwhelming to contemplate what was ahead as I felt so unworthy of God's blessing. What had we done to deserve our hearts desire being met through a pregnancy when so many had not had this longed for experience. Music was again a great escape during the pregnancy months as fear and anxiety could still creep in. We had lots of Alison Krauss (especially baby of mine) and Jonny Cash, artists that my dad listened to so this was comforting that even though he is no longer with us, there was still a link to the baby. Our old favourites "The sun will come out tomorrow" (from the musical Annie) and "my favourite things" (from the musical The Sound of Music) made me smile along with "you are my sunshine".

I was due in November 2019 and had 7 friends also having a baby in the September - October time so this was so lovely to have other girls at the same stage. Towards the end of the pregnancy, heartburn and back pain were unlike anything I have ever experienced but thankfully chiropractor and reflexology sessions were useful. My Nanny was too ill to travel on a planned holiday to Lake Como in Italy with my mum and auntie that summer in 2019 so I was gratefully nominated to take the ticket. However, swollen legs and ankles and extreme heat were not a great combination but again the forced rest was amazing. Unfortunately my lovely Nanny McIlveen (Annie) died suddenly from a fall in her home in mid October 2019, just a couple of weeks before I gave birth. This was very upsetting for the whole family and I couldn't believe that she would never meet the baby but came so close to doing so. The baby coming was a distraction for my mum and in the weeks ahead, I hope a comfort also as a new chapter had begun even though we didn't want to forget the old chapter.

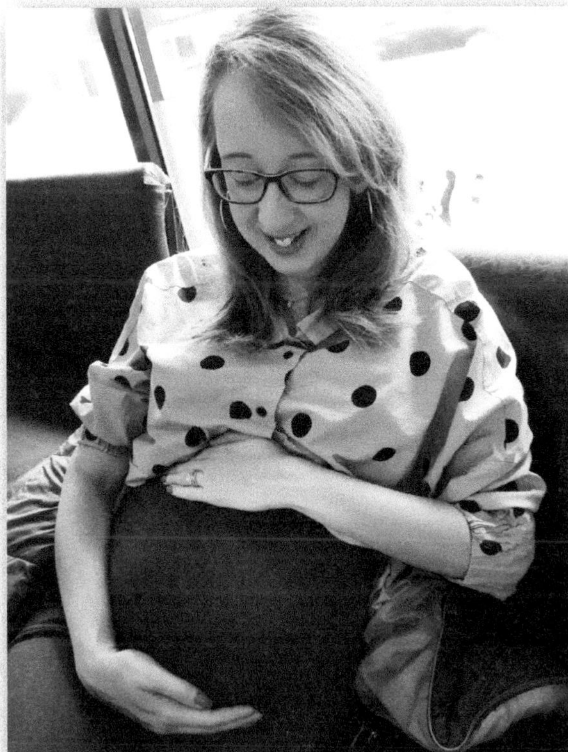

I was due for induction on the day before my due date but after arriving and getting sorted in hospital, we were told that the unit was too busy so did we mind moving to another hospital. We were just so grateful to be in this position of about to be having a baby that we would do anything so we happily drove up to the new hospital so uncertain of what was ahead but ridiculously excited. That Sunday was slow, Phil working away on his laptop at the side of the bed, just waiting. Looking back now, pre-pandemic, how things are so different and difficult now for anyone going through the same experience. Now all friendly smiles are unseen behind masks and a gentle touch of reassurance from a nurse is no longer the same.

It was soon confirmed to us that we were meant to have moved to that hospital as we were being looked after by a lovely midwife, who it transpired was on the IVF journey herself. I immediately felt that this was an angel as what a job to be doing with such care and love for others when your own heart was aching for the very thing you were working with and facing every day. It was touching to see her emotional after our birth and I pray that for that day it gave her hope rather than sadness for her own journey.

The birth and aftermath I found more traumatic than I thought. It just seemed to be more difficult and painful than I had anticipated. I was sick with the contractions and went in and out of consciousness with the medication but we got there in the end. At one stage there were 6 professionals in the room as things got a bit tense and the baby was stuck for what seemed like forever. When she was born I remember fainting and Phil having to hold her for a good bit after until I was transferred back to the ward as I felt so exhausted. She had the cord around her neck and her head was badly bruised so no wonder there was no crying for a while when she came out. I think like me, she was in a state of shock!

The relief that it was all over and she was here safely was something we will never forget. We had a few names picked for both genders after long discussions but nothing ever felt quite sure. After Nanny had died so recently, we wanted to incorporate her name if the baby was a girl. We decided on Annie-Rose Dorman Moody. Phil's granny was Rose and my great granny/great Auntie was Rose too so remains a family name. Dorman was my maiden name so in honour of my dad we wanted to acknowledge that side of the family who we remain close to. Her name is so special to us as it represents so many special people. She is often affectionately known as "The AR". Bringing this little bundle home was such a lovely experience as we played some encouraging worship music in the car to create a sense of calm and hope for her first car journey.

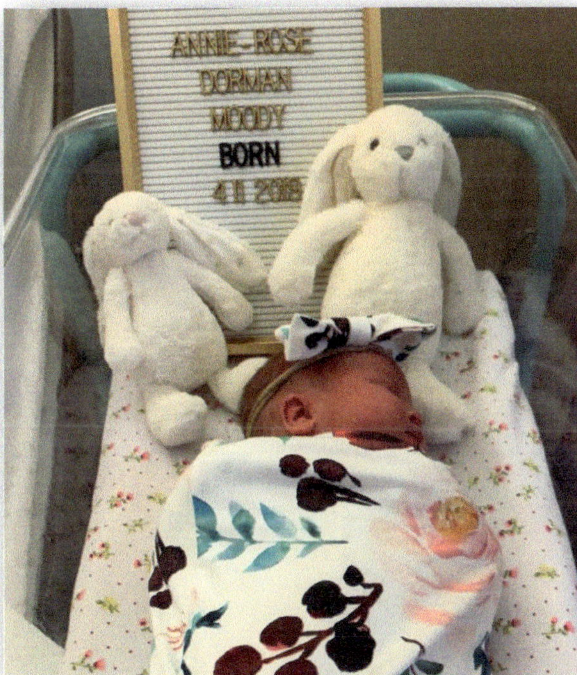

Not much is said about the aftermath and the recovery stage but it was physically a tough first week where pain, fatigue and weakness were my friends. I couldn't even talk about the labour for a few weeks without tears filling my eyes and yet it is many women's reality every day. I had nothing to compare it to but by the time I realised I was feeling worse than was normal it was too late as Mastitis had well set in which was pain like I've never felt before.

Thankfully the midwife persuaded the hospital to admit me again just a week after Annie-Rose was born which was the best thing as meant I had fast acting IV medication along with other things which helped the recovery process. However, I felt so unwell the first night in hospital that Phil had to take AR home overnight which was strange. From administering my own blood thinner injections, eating ice lollies in the middle of the night and being woken up at times every 15 minutes for observations, the 4 day experience was interesting but I was so thankful for a side room, a warm meal and plenty of prayers. It is the little things that we take for granted.

13
Tough Decisions

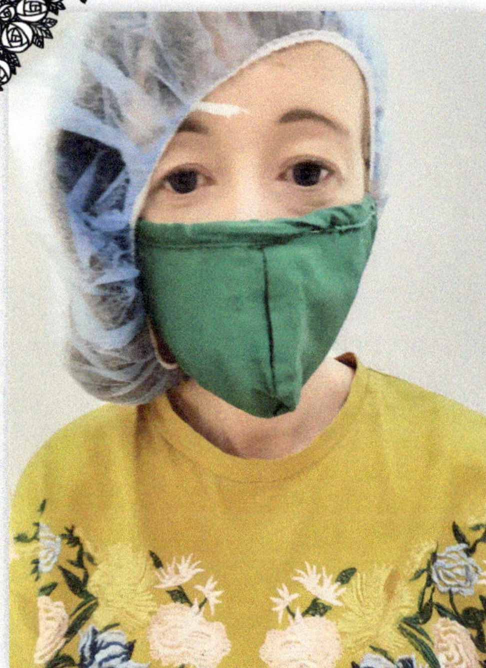

Proverbs 3 v 5

"Trust in the LORD with all your heart and lean not on your own understanding; in all your ways submit to him, and he will make your paths straight"

After those initial early weeks things were going well until on Christmas Eve Annie-Rose had to go into hospital due to bronchiolitis. Seeing her getting oxygen in A and E before moving to the children's ward was difficult and made more emotional by the fact that it was her first Christmas.

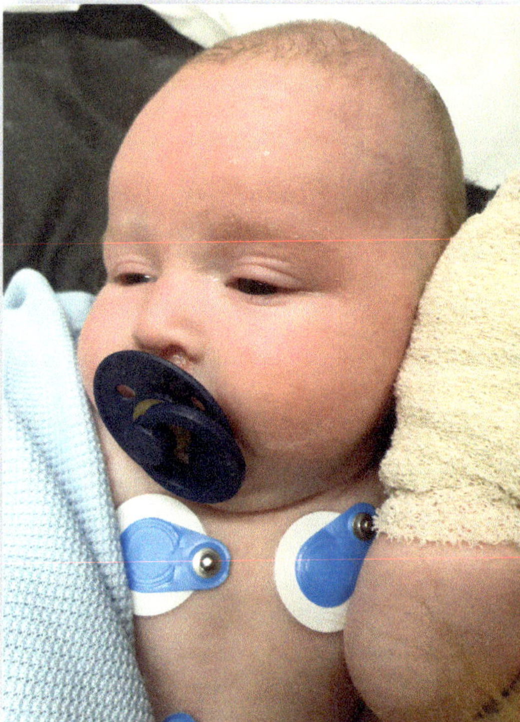

(Christmas Eve 2019)

Thankfully we got out on late on Christmas day but the experience made us appreciate and only imagine how difficult it must be to have a child who needed hospital stays for long periods of time and having to receive ongoing treatment. These parents are also often a forgotten group. Thankfully I finally got into the stride of maternity leave and enjoyed each day so much and still do with Annie-Rose. We enjoyed trying new things and new groups with most of our week filled with mums and tots groups, sensory class, baby cinema and library visits. Then in March 2020, the world stopped.

Corona virus/Covid 19 had arrived and changed all our lives. The pandemic forced us as a small family to slow down our running around and take time out which was a positive of what was happening amongst the anxiety and uncertainty about what was ahead. We had planned a dedication for Annie-Rose at church in mid-March and although it was not as we planned, it was a lovely service despite it being the last Sunday there would ever be church for months. It felt reassuring to know that whatever happened, she would be in God's hands, which we believed anyway.

We had one little frozen embryo straw sitting waiting to be kick started in Prague. We had always wanted a close gap between children if possible due to a few factors but now we were miles away and the world was a different place. We had tough decisions to make and it was easy to weigh it up in our own minds but we had to remember to include God in the conversation and accept the outcome. We had planned to go back to Prague just before Annie-Rose was one as I would still be off on maternity leave, we wouldn't have to pay for another year of storage at the clinic and I was getting older also.

There is such a strict time window which can change depending on medication impact and scan results etc. so there was a small opportunity in September when we thought if we don't do this now, travel restrictions may be imposed again or it could be another year until we had the opportunity. If it wasn't to work then we wanted to consider the next options in expanding our family as soon as possible. We got the necessary pre-treatment tests and scans and the medication ordered. With postal delays etc. there was a time of panic as if the medication did not arrive on time on a certain day then that was the chance missed. Thankfully it arrived in the morning of the day needed and we started the journey again for time '3.5ish' of IVF. We were very worried in the few weeks before travel as if we were in contact with someone with Covid, then we would have to isolate, resulting in us not being able to travel and missing this cycle. Then we got the news that Czech Republic was taken off the free travel corridor list and deemed as high risk/red which meant that we would have to isolate for 14 days upon return.

We decided that it was still worth it as the situation could be the same if not worse in a number of months and we had already started treatment. After deciding to commit, the next hurdle was trying to source flights. Flight timing opportunities had been reduced massively especially from Northern Ireland so none existed directly to Prague anymore. We only had to be in Prague for 2-3 days this time but flights were only running from Dublin twice a week at this point. Amazingly the two days that we required flights, they were running! At only half capacity, it meant Annie-Rose had her own seat without paying for it but travelling with a baby in a pandemic was uncomfortable.

We wanted to take her as it was a special place to us and hopefully to her in the future, but also if something happened and the borders were closed etc. at least we would all be together. It was scary and unknown. The airport in Prague was deserted with the majority of shops shut. I will never forget the feeling of walking around the airport on a Saturday afternoon with barely any people and no shops open. It was very surreal.

(first plane journey)

(Saturday afternoon in an airport September 2020)

In the end we were thankful that we took that small opportunity as a couple of weeks later, all flights to Prague were cancelled in Ireland and the borders were officially closed to tourists so again we could trust in God and thank Him for that timing. We were armed with our medical letter excusing our reason for travel which felt like some protection for the journey. Thankfully we knew the city well to have our bearings quickly and knew where to get food etc to get on with the next couple of days.

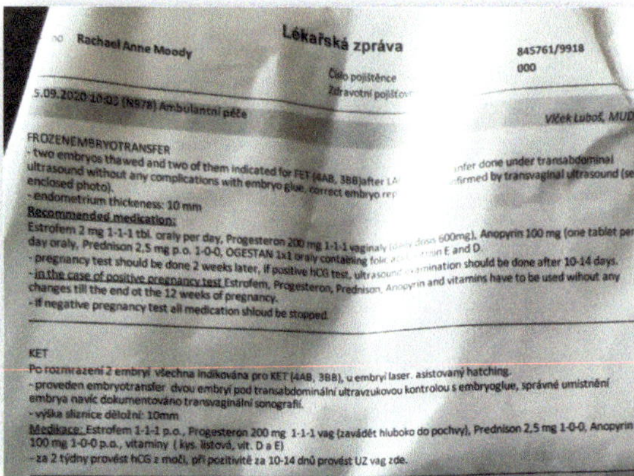

Rachael Anne Moody

Lékařská zpráva

Číslo pojištěnce 845761/9918

Zdravotní pojišťov[illegible] 000

5.09.2020 10:0[illegible] (N978) Ambulantní péče

Vlček Luboš, MUD[illegible]

FROZENEMBRYOTRANSFER

- two embryos thawed and two of them indicated for FET (4AB, 3BB)after [illegible] [illegible]nfer done under transabdominal ultrasound without any complications with embryo glue, correct embryo re[illegible] [illegible]firmed by transvaginal ultrasound (see enclosed photo).
- endometrium thickeness: 10 mm

__Recommended medication:__

Estrofem 2 mg 1-1-1 tbl. oraly per day, Progesteron 200 mg 1-1-1 vaginaly ([illegible] 600mg). Anopyrin 100 mg (one tablet per day oraly, Prednison 2,5 mg p.o. 1-0-0, OGESTAN 1x1 oraly containing fol[illegible] [illegible]in E and D.

- pregnancy test should be done 2 weeks later, if positive hCG test, ultrasoun[illegible] [illegible]amination should be done after 10-14 days.
- __in the case of positive pregnancy test__ Estrofem, Progesteron, Prednison, Anopyrin and vitamins have to be used wihout any changes till the end ot the 12 weeks of pregnancy.
- if negative pregnancy test all medication shloud be stopped.

KET

Po rozmrazení 2 embryí všechna indikována pro KET (4AB, 3BB), u embryí laser. asistovaný hatching.

- proveden embryotransfer dvou embryí pod transabdominální ultravzukovou kontrolou s embryoglue, správné umístnění embrya navíc dokumentováno transvaginální sonografií.
- výška sliznice děložní: 10mm

__Medikace:__ Estrofem 1-1-1 p.o., Progesteron 200 mg 1-1-1 vag (zavádět hluboko do pochvy), Prednison 2,5 mg 1-0-0, Anopyrin 100 mg 1-0-0 p.o., vitaminy (kys. listová, vit. D a E)

- za 2 týdny provést hCG z moči, při pozitivitě za 10-14 dnů provést UZ vag zde.

(Czech treatment schedule 3)

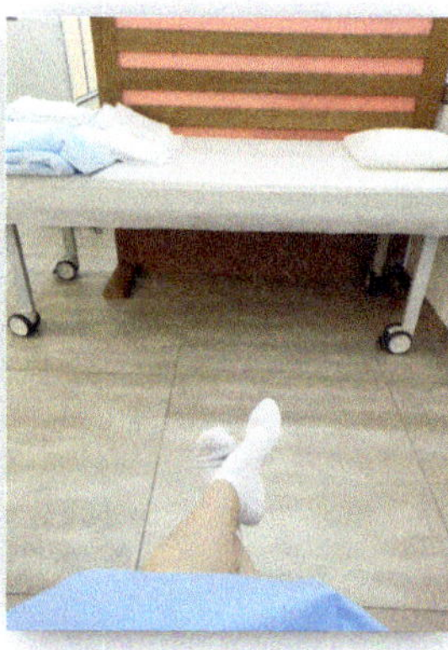

(familiar bays)

Everything went to plan at the clinic and again it was amazing to see potential life on a screen, waiting to be sustained. Even though it was a slightly lower graded embryo than before, there is always hope. The same tutu and trainer socks greeted me again. We followed the clinic with our usual tradition of visiting the garden centre then the shopping mall. There is something about walking around shops in a new country that is strangely distracting. In the blink of an eye we were back on the mask wearing plane and home again where the famous familiar two week wait began. This time it was different as there were no distractions with work or walks or laughs with friends, we had to all isolate due to foreign travel for 14 days.

By the end of this time, we would know the outcome. We had to make our own entertainment in our bubble of 3. It was lovely for Phil to get proper time with Annie-Rose and each night we spent time together on mini dates at home. Time like that is memory making. We were able to distract ourselves by de-cluttering each room in the house and trying not to think of the upcoming pregnancy test to determine the end of the road or a happy beginning. We were both secretly hoping for twins yet again. The day came and despite being through this process other times before, I could barely sleep. I didn't have a strong intuition one way or the other but did have a sense of peace that we could cope with whatever happened. Gratitude also overwhelmed as I watched a sleeping Annie-Rose during this time.

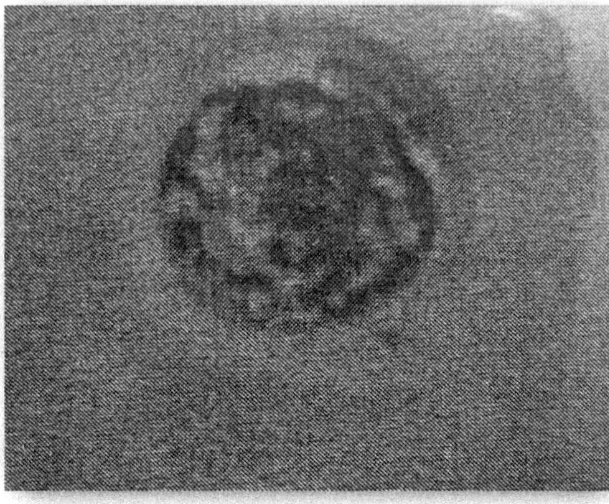

(another potential little one)

And there it was, even after trying a few different branded tests, the outcome was the same. No second line. I had forgotten how painful it was to have a failed result. Initial feelings of guilt crept in that you feel your body has failed to sustain the little embryos which was followed by sorrow. Sorrow surrounded that this was likely the final end of the road. We had decided that we would not try the process again as never mind the financial reasons, it was physically rough on your body with all the medication and who knew ethically as you could end up with a large number of eggs and the situation may be never ending. We took it as a natural time to stop and felt God was in that with us.

Despite the tears, having Annie-Rose forced us to keep going and even the simple things like getting out of bed and eating came much more naturally this time because she was here. Our hearts just broke that she would unlikely have siblings and we would be unable to have the 3 or 4 children that we desired. The bigger picture was that she was the beautiful blessing and how amazing it was that she was entrusted to us *"for such a time as this"*. A few verses stuck with me during this time including Psalm 61 v 2, *"When my heart is overwhelmed, lead me to the rock that is higher than I"*. We believe God is in control but there are times when emotions take over. "When" indicates a permission to feel overwhelmed so we are allowed to feel that way in our own personal circumstances. In these times, we can cry out to the Holy Spirit to lead us to the rock that is higher above it all. A rock signifies strength, something secure and steadfast that will remain with us. Jesus leads us to that higher ground where our perspective can change as He promises to help us walk above or through our difficult circumstances with us. Another simple and well known verse that has always stayed with me and served as a reminder on this occasion was *"Cast all your cares upon Him, because He cares for you"*.

We have been instructed to 'cast' our anxieties full force onto God, he can handle it. Our natural instinct may be anger or frustration in our circumstances. Thanking God or seeking peace in our broken situation may not be our initial response always. This is something that the IVF process has helped me be more proactive with, trying not to lose peace over things that I cannot control. These verses have helped me focus on God's promises of peace. He cares, He is always there high above our circumstances, He is unchanging and will provide enough light for each step that we take. As a result, we should remain thankful.

14
Keep Looking Up

1 John 3:1

"See what kind of love the Father has given to us, that we should be called children of God; and so we are."

So what of the future. Somewhere on this journey I was reminded in Genesis 30v 2 that *"Then God remembered Rachel; he listened to her and enabled her to conceive."* Maybe this will be my story and my ending or maybe not. At times we thought maybe this pregnancy won't be fulfilled but it was. No matter the future, we need to move forward looking upwards, not backwards or sideward's. We are told to lean on Christ in the storm, easier said than done but we should be thankful that we have someone to lean on who will carry us in our sorrow. Fertility struggles are like an invisible weight around your neck, noticed by only a few who you have confided in. It makes you weak physically, mentally, emotionally and spiritually but Christ alone remains the cornerstone, weak made strong, through the storm He is Lord of all. Adoption will also be on our hearts and I pray God intensifies this desire or removes it as His will reveals.

We have been adopted into God's family and now we have chosen to go on this journey to hopefully meet our little lives ahead and welcome them into our own family. We believe that God will answer our prayer for more children in our lives but only He knows how. Mr and Mrs Moody don't know what the future holds but how amazing that we know who holds the future and we must remember to thank Him, praise Him and love Him wholeheartedly no matter the outcome.

These little soldiers are on my dressing table and serve as a daily visual reminder that even though I may let God down each day, he will always protect me. He goes before us into battles, but He also protects and surrounds us, allowing us to always lean on him from behind. No matter what the battle is that you are facing, the battle belongs to the Lord. We can lean on the assurance that even though we are "weak and heavy laden", what a friend we have in Jesus! He calls us to *"come to me, all you who are weary and burdened, and I will give you rest"* (Matthew 11:28).

Fostering or adoption has always been on my heart and it has not strayed from that place. We both understand that this process can take a couple of years of intense assessments and more emotional upheaval but it is the path we would like to pursue. We investigated this recently but unfortunately got the news that we had to wait at least a year from a failed IVF procedure before pursuing this process. This was gutting as we had wanted to keep going as we feel we have a home here which we want to open as soon as possible to other children who need it. But again, God is in control despite our disappointments, we have to keep trusting and looking up and hope that our desires meet God's for the future. If they don't, then we believe that God meets us where we are no matter what.

Another future hurdle is what, when and how to communicate this journey with Annie-Rose. This was a big motivation for completing the book to help explain, when needed, our hearts at this time and how much she is loved. We have had some special times over the course of 3 lockdowns since she was born including dressing her up for zoom quiz rounds, long country walks exploring Cullybackey and appearing in a cbeebies programme together. She brings an overload of joy each day and we pray that she grows up to reflect the meaning of her name as being "gracious" and "merciful". Hopefully one day we will have the blended family desired or maybe not and that will be ok too. She is more than enough.

IVF was our choice, it will not be everyone's and we may never know if it was God's will or our desire that led us on this path but we do feel a peace at present for our journey but only God knows the bigger picture. We are thankful that

God is a God of peace "Jehovah-Shalom". All we can do is ask for forgiveness if this was indeed our own selfish path. We need to remember to praise Him in the storm as well as thank Him for His daily blessings and grace far beyond what we will ever deserve. It is well with our souls when we seek God fully in any circumstance. We are thankful for this journey and all that we have learnt along the way. God is already ahead whatever the next chapter may be. My heart will always break for other couples going along this same path. No matter if IVF was the right choice or not, it has thrown us both into the arms of Jesus and that can never be a bad thing.

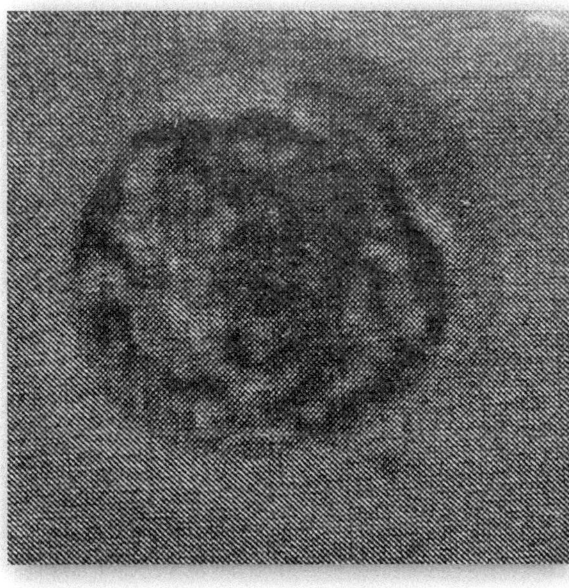

(Beginning of the process...)

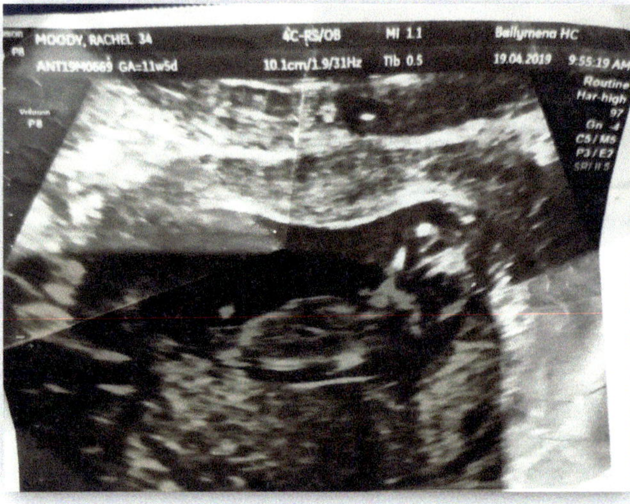

(Middle of the process...)

(End of the process!)

A note from Phil

Ecclesiastes 3:1-8

"To everything there is a season and a time to every purpose under the heaven".

On reflection of the journey described so brilliantly by Rachael, I wanted to add a few words for men going through similar situations. During this time you will never be able to comprehend the sacrificial love your partner gives at this time.

The verse above has always been my strength throughout this journey. From a young age, we hear of stories such as Amy Carmichael where prayers are always aimed at getting a particular result. But, as we know, God often has different plans that we are not aware of. Only upon going through these events can the true nature be revealed. When praying regarding starting our family, it was always a focus of mine to not ask could we have a child but rather to ask that God would let us know the journey planned for us, no matter how heartbreaking this could end up being. This verse provides hope that if we were to have a family that this would be in God's timing and not of our own biological mindset even though our hearts desired it so much.

Most people would describe me as a realistic person. Sometimes it has been hard in the journey to find areas of hope, but seeing Rachael go through so much selflessly encouraged me to search for hope in the hard times described.

Thinking back to my first hospital visit where I was greeted by a recently graduated nurse speaking bashfully to me about how to "deposit the specimen" in the container being careful not to spill any, is all but an unfortunate life event to have to go through. After the event you become self conscious knowing people know what has happened, but hopefully moving forward the stigma around this will become removed.

This experience has proven difficult, however it is only with a strong marriage and trust in God that allows you to find the hope in the dark situation, the ability to change a negative situation into a possibility, the opportunity to discover things about yourself and your partner that only this process will provide and finally, a knowledge that God's love is amazing and indescribable.

On the day of getting to hold Annie-Rose, I could feel God's presence near, knowing that such a precious gift came from our trust in Him. It was comforting to know that this was our season and that His encouragement in dark times of 'the following spring' had come to fruition.

Before starting this journey my naivety into the complex mind of a female in relation to the feelings attached to the process of starting a family cannot be fathomed. Often simple sayings such as "when will you be having kids?" or "will you be next?" can cause such undue pain in individual's lives and often cannot be understood to those not in similar situations.

One of my key learning's from this process has been not to stay silent and be ashamed. Infertility in couples is becoming more and more prevalent each year and it is becoming a problem that requires a voice to help those uneducated to understand the key issues. When chatting to friends about the process, I was encouraged that when I was open regarding the steps that this was met with a true desire to try and fathom the emotional, physical and spiritual needs of both Rachael and I. Having gone through many pregnancy announcements coinciding with times of pain, it can be difficult to hide your anguish and share in the celebration of others. This was most notable for me during a summer holiday with friends who had just announced their happy news. It was surprising to myself how the devil uses opportunities like this to challenge your faith and I have to admit that at times I let him win. Only through knowing that friends and family are there for you in the tough times as well as Rachael's continuing love always guides you back to a positive place.

Annie-Rose reminds me every day of the blessed situation our journey has resulted in and I am always thankful knowing this could have been so different given the circumstances Rachael described. Often I selfishly think we could just repeat the process again but through the creation of this book it has helped remind me of the love and care and toll that this had on Rachael and that this has to be considered in any decisions moving forward. Rachael has spoken regarding fostering and adoption options and again this alongside the continuing chance of a naturally conceived child or the potential to repeat the process is something that as a couple, we will continue to put in God's hand and allow Him to continue to help us understand the possibilities ahead.

No words will ever comprehend Rachael's sacrifices and selfless love to allow Annie-Rose to enter the world and for this I will be forever grateful to her for giving me the opportunity to become a father to such a life loving, comedic Dada's girl that brings me such joy each day. I look forward to continuing our journey and understanding what lies ahead for our family.

Time out for practical, self-care ideas....

- Go for a walk whether rain or shine
- Listen to music
- Journal, make notes, document happy and sad moments
- Try alternative therapies e.g. calming essential oils, acupuncture, aromatherapy and reflexology
- Make a list and think about what activities make to you smile and do them
- Get a good box set going to serve as a distraction, with popcorn and treats too of course.
- Clear your schedule and just say no!
- Comfort food within limits but sometimes you just need to eat that tub of ice-cream and have a good cry.
- Try for 5 minutes of golden time daily even if it just putting on an eye mask for 5 minutes and zoning out.
- Talk and never feel you are a burden by doing so. True friends will listen.
- Get stuck into a Bible study, the more time spend immersed will start to fill your heart with joy again.
- Plan happy dates with your friends or partner and do something fun.
- Get a bear hug, deep pressure can be soothing.
- Try a new hobby, that thing you've always wanted to try or even doing a bit of research on something can be therapeutic as your thoughts are transported elsewhere.
- Declutter wardrobes and clean cupboards in your house can be the ultimate distraction and it is productive too!

- Talk to others who have been there, reach out on social media or in person.
- Try counselling and see if it is for you.
- Rest - fill your cup again with energy.
- Take one day at a time, everything in its time.
- Stock up on vitamins and iron hits to make sure you are physically at your best.
- Overall, maintain a good diet to fuel you when feeling low.
- Cook or bake, everyone will be happy to taste the offerings!

Playlist of hope and encouragement

I have this hope (Tenth Avenue North)
Worn (Tenth Avenue North)
I look to you (Selah)
One thing I know (Selah)
I will carry you (Selah)
Just be held (Casting Crowns)
Somewhere in your silent night (Casting Crowns)
Oh my soul (Casting Crowns)
Even if (Mercy me)
King of my heart (Kutless)
O come all you unfaithful (Sovereign Grace)
Rescue (Lauren Daigle)
He will hold me fast (Keith & Kristyn Getty)
My heart is filled with thankfulness (Keith & Kristyn Getty)
Shepherd (CityAlight)
God is for us (CityAlight)
Christ is mine forevermore (CityAlight)
Yet not I but through Christ in me (CityAlight)
Sovereign over us (Aaron Keys)
It is well (Bethel music)
Goodness of God (Bethel music)
Belovedness (Sarah Kroger)
Thy will be done (Hillary Scott)
When the rain comes (Third Day)
Great is Thy Faithfulness
How can a moment last forever (Celine Dion)
The Prayer (Josh Groban)

Journaling images

it is worthless and ...
end is to be burned.
[9] Though we speak in this way, yet in your case, beloved, we feel sure of better things—things that belong to salvation. [10] For God is not unjust so as to overlook your work and the love that you have shown for his name in serving the saints, as you still do. [11] And we desire each one of you to show the same earnestness to have the full assurance of hope until the end, [12] so that you may not be sluggish, but imitators of those who through faith and patience inherit the promises.

The Certainty of God's Promise

[13] For when God made a promise to Abraham, since he had no one greater by whom to swear, he swore by himself, [14] saying, "Surely I will bless you and multiply you." [15] And thus Abraham, having patiently waited, obtained the promise. [16] For people swear by something greater than themselves, and in all their disputes an oath is final for confirmation. [17] So when God desired to show more convincingly to the heirs of the promise the unchangeable character of his purpose, he guaranteed it with an oath, [18] so that by two unchangeable things, in which it is impossible for God to lie, we who have fled for refuge might have strong encouragement to hold fast to the hope set before us. [19] We have this as a sure and steadfast anchor of the soul, a hope that enters into the inner place behind the curtain, [20] where Jesus has gone as a forerunner on our behalf, having become a high priest forever after the order of Melchizedek.

The Priestly Order of Melchizedek

7 For this Melchizedek, king of Salem, priest of the Most High God, met Abraham returning from the slaughter of the kings and blessed him, [2] and to him Abraham apportioned a tenth part of everything. He is first, by translation of his name, king of righteousness, and then he is also king of Salem, that is, king of peace. [3] He is without father or mother or genealogy, having neither beginning of days nor end of life, but resembling the Son of God he continues a priest forever.

[4] See how great this man was to whom Abraham the patriarch gave a tenth of the spoils! [5] And those descendants of Levi who receive the priestly office have a commandment in the law to take tithes from the people, that is, from their brothers, though these also are

tithes from Abra...
had the promises...
the inferior is bles...
one case tithes are...
in the other case, b...
that he lives. [9] On...
himself, who recei...
Abraham, [10] for h...
ancestor when M...

Jesus Compared ...

[11] Now if per...
through the Lev...
the people recei...
would there hav...
after the order o...
named after th...
there is a chang...
essarily a chang...
of whom these...
another tribe, f...
at the altar. [14] F...
descended fro...
that tribe Mos...
[15] This bec...
another pries...
chizedek, [16] w...
basis of a leg...
descent, but...
life. [17] For it i...

"You are...
after...

[18] For on the...
is set aside b...
ness [19] (for t...
on the othe...
through w...
[20] And it...
who form...
without a...
priest with...

"The L...
an...
'You a...

[22] This m...
covenant...
[23] The...
because t...
tinuing i...

"Our Father in heaven,
hallowed be your name.
Your kingdom come,
your will be done,
on earth as it is in heaven.
Give us this day our daily bread,
and forgive us our debts,
as we also have forgiven our debtors.
And lead us not into temptation,
but deliver us from evil.
For if you forgive others their trespasses, your heavenly Father will also forgive you, but if you do not forgive others their trespasses, neither will your Father forgive your trespasses.
Fasting
"And when you fast, do not look gloomy like the hypocrites, for they disfigure their faces that their fasting may be seen by others. Truly, I say to you, they have received their reward. But when you fast, anoint your head and wash your face, that your fasting may not be seen by others but by your Father who is in secret. And your Father who sees in secret will reward you.
Lay Up Treasures in Heaven
"Do not lay up for yourselves treasures on earth, where moth and rust destroy and where thieves break in and steal, but lay up for yourselves treasures in heaven, where neither moth nor rust destroys and where thieves do not break in and steal. For where your treasure is, there your heart will be also.
"The eye is the lamp of the body. So, if your eye is healthy, your whole body will be full of light, but if your eye is bad, your whole body will be full of darkness. If then the light in you is darkness, how great is the darkness!
"No one can serve two masters, for either he will hate the one and love the other, or he will be devoted to the one and despise the other. You cannot serve God and money.
Do Not Be Anxious
"Therefore I tell you, do not be anxious about your life, what you will eat or what you will drink, nor about your body, what you will put on. Is not life more than food, and the body more than clothing? Look at the birds of the air: they neither sow nor reap nor gather into barns, and yet your heavenly Father feeds
811
thy will be done
IVF

LAMENTATIONS
65 You will give them dullness of heart;
your curse will be on them.
66 You will pursue them in anger and
destroy them
from under your heavens, O LORD.
The Holy Stones Lie Scattered
4 How the gold has grown dim,
how the pure gold is changed!
The holy stones lie scattered
at the head of every street.
2 The precious sons of Zion,
worth their weight in fine gold,
how they are regarded as earthen pots,
the work of a potter's hands!
3 Even jackals offer the breast;
they nurse their young;
but the daughter of my people has become
cruel,
like the ostriches in the wilderness.
4 The tongue of the nursing infant sticks
to the roof of its mouth for thirst;
the children beg for food,
but no one gives to them.
5 Those who once feasted on delicacies
perish in the streets;
those who were brought up in purple
embrace ash heaps.
6 For the chastisement of the daughter of
my people has been greater
than the punishment of Sodom,
which was overthrown in a moment,
and no hands were wrung for her.
7 Her princes were purer than snow,
whiter than milk;
their bodies were more ruddy than coral,
the beauty of their form was like sap-
phire.
8 Now their face is blacker than soot;
they are not recognized in the streets;
their skin has shriveled on their bones;
it has become as dry as wood.
9 Happier were the victims of the sword
than the victims of hunger,
who wasted away, pierced
by lack of the fruits of the field.
10 The hands of compassionate women
have boiled their own children;
THE LORD IS
my portion
689

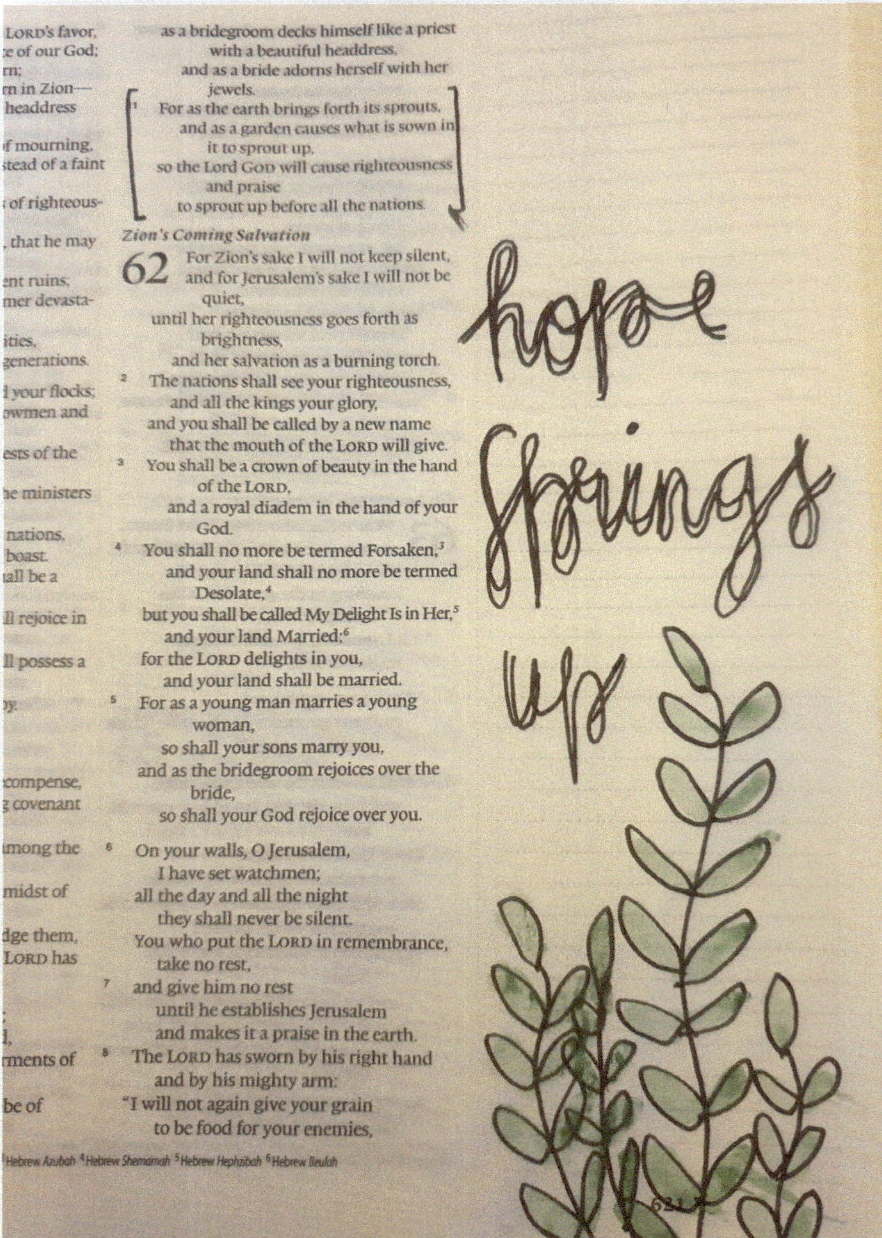

as a bridegroom decks himself like a priest
with a beautiful headdress,
and as a bride adorns herself with her
jewels.
11 For as the earth brings forth its sprouts,
and as a garden causes what is sown in
it to sprout up,
so the Lord GOD will cause righteousness
and praise
to sprout up before all the nations.

Zion's Coming Salvation

62 For Zion's sake I will not keep silent,
and for Jerusalem's sake I will not be
quiet,
until her righteousness goes forth as
brightness,
and her salvation as a burning torch.
2 The nations shall see your righteousness,
and all the kings your glory,
and you shall be called by a new name
that the mouth of the LORD will give.
3 You shall be a crown of beauty in the hand
of the LORD,
and a royal diadem in the hand of your
God.
4 You shall no more be termed Forsaken,[3]
and your land shall no more be termed
Desolate,[4]
but you shall be called My Delight Is in Her,[5]
and your land Married;[6]
for the LORD delights in you,
and your land shall be married.
5 For as a young man marries a young
woman,
so shall your sons marry you,
and as the bridegroom rejoices over the
bride,
so shall your God rejoice over you.

6 On your walls, O Jerusalem,
I have set watchmen;
all the day and all the night
they shall never be silent.
You who put the LORD in remembrance,
take no rest,
7 and give him no rest
until he establishes Jerusalem
and makes it a praise in the earth.
8 The LORD has sworn by his right hand
and by his mighty arm:
"I will not again give your grain
to be food for your enemies,

[3] Hebrew *Azubah* [4] Hebrew *Shemamah* [5] Hebrew *Hephzibah* [6] Hebrew *Beulah*

ISAIAH 11:10

11 In that day the Lord will extend his hand
yet a second time to recover the remnant that
remains of his people, from Assyria, from
Egypt, from Pathros, from Cush,[1] from Elam,
from Shinar, from Hamath, and from the coast-
lands of the sea.

12 He will raise a signal for the nations
and will assemble the banished of Israel,
and gather the dispersed of Judah
from the four corners of the earth.
13 The jealousy of Ephraim shall depart,
and those who harass Judah shall be cut
off;
Ephraim shall not be jealous of Judah,
and Judah shall not harass Ephraim.
14 But they shall swoop down on the shoul-
der of the Philistines in the west,
and together they shall plunder the
people of the east.
They shall put out their hand against
Edom and Moab,
and the Ammonites shall obey them.
15 And the LORD will utterly destroy[2]
the tongue of the Sea of Egypt,
and will wave his hand over the River
with his scorching breath,[3]
and strike it into seven channels,
and he will lead people across in san-
dals.
16 And there will be a highway from Assyria
for the remnant that remains of his
people,
as there was for Israel
when they came up from the land of
Egypt.

The LORD Is My Strength and My Song

12 You[1] will say in that day:
"I will give thanks to you, O LORD,
for though you were angry with me,
your anger turned away,

I will trust, and will not be afraid;
for the LORD GOD[5] is my strength and my
song,
and he has become my salvation."
3 With joy you[6] will draw water from the
wells of salvation.

The Judgment of Babylon

13 The oracle concerning Babylon which
Isaiah the son of Amoz saw.

I know that my Redeemer Lives
JOB 19:25
For I know that my Redeemer lives,
and at the last he will stand upon the earth.

Some infertility acronyms

- tip of the iceberg basics covered

2WW/TWW	Two-week wait (the time between ovulation and either a period or a positive pregnancy test)
BFN	Big fat negative (negative result on a pregnancy test)
BFP	Big fat positive (positive result on a pregnancy test)
CP	Chemical pregnancy
hCG	Human chorionic gonadotrophin (the hormone that pregnancy tests measure)
MC	Miscarriage
OH	Other half
OTD	Official test day
OHSS	Ovarian hyperstimulation syndrome
PCOS	Polycystic ovary syndrome
PG	Pregnant
Rainbow baby	A baby born after losing a pregnancy or a child
SA	Semen analysis (an assessment of sperm quantity, quality, and motility)
TTC	Trying to conceive
Frostie	Frozen embryo
IVF	In vitro fertilization
ICSI	Intra-cytoplasmic sperm injection
IUI	Intrauterine insemination

Please get in touch if you have any further questions or ever need a listening ear on your own journey. I would love to hear from you.

rdorman01@qub.ac.uk

* 9 7 8 1 6 4 9 6 0 1 9 4 0 *

BV - #0130 - 151121 - C48 - 215/143/6 - PB - 9781649601940 - Gloss Lamination